PRESSING ON: UNSTABLE APPROACH CONTINUATION BIAS

How Pilots Risk Landing Accidents and What Can Be Done About It

© 2021 Edwin Vincent Odisho II

All rights reserved. No part of this publication may be reproduced or transmitted in any form or by any means, electronic or mechanical, including photocopy, recording, or any information storage and retrieval system, without permission in writing from the publisher.

Requests for permission to make copies of any part of this work should be submitted online at EdOdisho@gmail.com

Cover art by Eyewitness Animations, http://eyewitnessanimations.com/

The thoughts, opinions, and attitudes expressed in this work are my own, and do not represent those of my employer.

ISBN 978-1-950183-90-6

AUTHOR'S NOTE

This book is based on original research I did while pursuing a PhD in Aviation at Embry-Riddle Aeronautical University. As I considered various topics for my dissertation, I realized that it was important for me to address a real-world aviation problem, hopefully solving one that had plagued airline operations for years. Although I explored several potential topics that met my criteria, I eventually selected one consistently challenging aviation safety practitioners, governmental regulators, and airline pilot training program managers in recent times.

Unstable approaches have been a hot topic in aviation safety circles for years. There are a plethora of National Transportation Safety Board reports describing accidents resulting from runway excursions (a veer off or overrun from the runway surface) and/or collision with terrain caused by pilots continuing an unstable approach to a landing attempt. Following a series of airline accidents caused in part by this phenomenon, in 2003 the Federal Aviation Administration developed stabilized approach criteria for airlines to use in their pilot training and standard operating procedures aviation safety programs. These stabilized approach criteria were developed for pilots to assess aircraft performance in the approach and landing phases of flight and to provide guidance for pilots to perform a rejected landing, or missed approach, if these criteria were exceeded. In spite of these efforts, the risk mitigation strategies for airlines to reduce runway excursion and/or collision with terrain have fallen short of expectations. Incidents such as Asiana 214 and PK8303 are recent examples of accidents that would have been prevented had pilots adhered to standard operating procedures developed to mitigate the risk associated with continuing an unstable approach to a landing attempt.

This book is based on my doctoral research, *Predicting Pilot Risk Misperception of Runway Excursion Risk Through Machine Learning Algorithms of Recorded Flight Data*. The National Aeronautics and Space Administration made a set of recorded flight data available for public research. These data were collected from a fleet of airliners while operating in the United States National Airspace System. I was able to use these data in my research and analyze the data for evidence of unstable approaches. I also used these data to develop predictive models to determine the probability of occurrence of the phenomena just described. I invented a new term, *Unstable Approach Risk Misperception* (UARM), to represent this event. The acronym UARM is used to represent the lapse in pilot aeronautical decision making that occurs when a pilot elects to continue an unstable approach to a landing attempt, rather than performing a rejected landing, thus risking a runway excursion and/or collision with terrain.

Questions arise when one attempts to address this aviation problem. How often do unstable approaches occur? Why do pilots seemingly accept risk associated with unstable approaches and make the decision to continue an unstable approach to landing? If unstable approaches are risky, why do a very high percentage of unstable approaches result in seemingly acceptable landings? How can the occurrence of the continuation bias regarding unstable approaches and risk of runway excursion and/or collision with terrain be prevented? Could the development of new pilot display technology be used to alert pilots to an impending unstable approach and simplify the rejected landing decision making process? I have addressed each of these concerns and present solutions to this important aviation problem.

Pressing On

It is my hope that my efforts to solve this problem can assist key aviation policy makers and airline pilot training managers in the development of new and innovative risk mitigation strategies regarding the attempt to reduce that probability of accidents or incidents regarding runway excursions and/or collision with terrain following an unstable approach.

In this work, I present my original research, and propose a solution to this aviation problem that has been a hot topic for years. I have developed a method to not only predict the probability of UARM, but also how to use this ability to mitigate the risk of runway excursion and/or collision with terrain. For the reader interested in a more detailed description of those areas of my research, I would respectfully suggest that you reference my dissertation on which this work is based. My complete dissertation can be found at the following link: https://commons.erau.edu/edt/503/.

SYNOPSIS

The topic of this book focuses on one aspect of risk associated with runway excursion and/or collision with terrain that occurs when a pilot elects to continue an unstable approach to a landing attempt. There are many reasons why unstable approaches occur and also just as many reasons pilots use to justify *pressing on* to landing when faced with evidence of an unstable approach. Why would a pilot accept risk of an accident or incident when deciding to *press on* when faced with evidence of an unstable approach? The Flight Safety Foundation lists several potential reasons for pilots *pressing on* to landing even after they have realized that one or more stable approach criteria have not been exceeded. Examples include issues such as fatigue, ATC flow control, and company or management pressure. Many operational issues can influence the circumstances affecting the stability of an approach.

The FSF and other aviation entities offer mitigation strategies for pilots to use to not only prevent the occurrence of an unstable approach, but also the tools to analyze and assess aircraft performance in the approach and landing phases of fight. FAA guidelines and airline standard operating procedures (SOPs) mandate that the result of this assessment should be a rejected landing when a pilot realizes stabilized approach criteria have not been met.

The results of my research indicate that even though unstable approaches are relatively rare (about 4% of all approaches in the NAS), once they do occur, a rejected landing only occurs approximately 5% of the time. Why do pilots almost all universally *press on* when they fly an unstable approach? More importantly, how can this lapse in aeronautical decision-making be corrected and prevented? The results of my research not only demonstrate an ability to predict the probability of occurrence of this risky behavior, but provide opportunities to develop safety risk mitigation strategies to prevent it.

Follow along as I describe how widespread the problem of UARM is in the airline industry, how previous safety risk mitigation strategies have not been successful, and how my research provides a path forward to eliminate the problem of pilots *pressing on* to landing during an unstable approach. What this book does *not* provide are reasons why unstable approaches occur and how other influences such as weather, ATC processes, CRM, or pilot-machine interface affect the pilot's ability to fly a stabilized approach. Thus, the topic of this book does not address the causes or reasons for the unstable approach, but rather how pilots can be provided the tools to reduce the likelihood of UARM and the resulting risk of runway excursion and/or collision with terrain when they face evidence of an unstable approach.

CONTENTS

Author's Note iii
Synopsis vi
Unstable approaches and pilot risk perception 1
    Regulatory Guidance for Stabilized Approaches 6
Research overview 18
    Identifying the Aviation Problem 24
    Purpose of the Research 25
    Significance of the Study 26
    Research Questions 27
    Delimitations 27
    Limitations and Assumptions 28
    Summary 29
Discussion, conclusions, and recommendations 31
    Discussion 32
    Conclusions 45
    Limitations of the findings 51
    Recommendations 51
Aviation research using mining techniques 56
    Data mining methods 56
    Text mining methods 60
    Machine learning predictive models 62
    Unanswered Questions in Aviation Research 89
    Summary 96
Moving forward 98
Appendix 101
    Research Methodology 101
    Data Coding and Algorithm Development 108
    Data Analysis Results 112
Definitions 120
Acronyms 122
References 124
Acknowledgements 134
About the author 135

PRESSING ON: UNSTABLE APPROACH CONTINUATION BIAS

How Pilots Risk Landing Accidents and What Can Be Done about It

Captain Edwin Odisho PhD

Miami FL

January 2021

Rocket Science Publishing

UNSTABLE APPROACHES AND PILOT RISK PERCEPTION

On 22 May 2020, Flight PK 8303, an A320 operated by Pakistan International Airlines, approached Jinnah International Airport in Karachi, Pakistan for an approach and landing to runway 25L. The aircraft was descending way too high and fast to comply with stable approach guidelines. Rather than perform a rejected landing, as recommended by governmental regulatory agencies, and mandated by the carrier's SOPs, the captain elected to continue the unstable approach to a landing attempt. In addition to being high and fast, the A320 was also not configured for landing (landing gear not down).

The unstable approach resulted in the aircraft touching down on the runway with the engine nacelles, significantly damaging both engines. As the aircraft settled onto the runway, the captain began at first to apply braking and reverse thrust, but then suddenly and inexplicably, reversed his decision to land and advanced the thrust levers to go-around power to execute a rejected landing. Once airborne, the A320 quickly experienced a dual engine failure due to the damage sustained on the landing attempt and crashed into a neighborhood near the airport. The crash killed 97 out of the 99 souls on board (AAIBP, 2020). This accident could have been prevented had the crew followed SOPs, yet the crew elected to continue the landing attempt even when faced with evidence of an unstable approach. Could this accident have been predicted and therefore, prevented?

My research indicates that not only could this tragedy have been predicted with a very high predictive power, but also prevented based on better pilot training programs, among other things. Additionally, recently developed pilot avionic alerting technologies could be implemented on commercial aircraft flight decks which warn pilots of an unstable approach and an impending risk of runway excursion. These developments in training and technology would help to ensure that landing accidents caused by unstable approaches no longer put passengers and the traveling public in harm's way.

The Federal Aviation Administration (FAA), the National Transportation Safety Board (NTSB), the Flight Safety Foundation (FSF), and the International Air Transport Association (IATA) have identified the continuation of an unstable approach to a landing as a hazard that has contributed to runway excursion (RE) accidents and incidents. The FAA (2003) defined a RE as a landing attempt that results in an overrun or veer off the runway surface. The IATA Accident database indicated that 61% of all aviation accidents from 2012-2016 occurred during the approach and landing phases of flight. IATA also claimed that 16% of those accidents contained unstable approach contributory factors (IATA, 2017).

Consequently, the NTSB has issued numerous safety recommendations to enhance runway safety, which have been consistently included in recent NTSB Most Wanted List of Transportation Safety Improvements (NTSB, 2019a). A review of recent NTSB accident investigation reports produced evidence that aircraft operators have not fully developed effective risk mitigation strategies concerning REs (FAA, 2014, 2015; NTSB, 2000, 2001, 2014a, 2014b, 2016, 2019b).

The background on stable approaches began in 1997 with NTSB Safety Recommendation A-97-85 that requested the FAA require all 14 CFR Part 121 and 135 operators to provide guidance for pilots regarding critical safety-of-flight decision-making, particularly regarding stabilized approaches. A Part 121 air carrier (i.e. airliners) is an alias for scheduled passenger/freight operations and a Part 135 carrier comprises only commuter and on-demand operations. In response to the NTSB recommendations, the FAA issued Flight Standards Handbook Bulletin for Air Transportation (HBAT) 98-22, *stabilized approaches*. A key component of this document was the requirement for all 14 CFR Part 121 and 135 operators to establish defined criteria for stabilized approaches and also to train pilots to perform rejected landings if stabilized approach conditions were not met (NTSB, 2001). Although unstable approaches were also a known hazard with general aviation (GA) aircraft, these operators were considered out of scope because data have only been obtained for a Part 121 carrier.

Despite these initiatives, American Airlines flight 1420 crashed during a landing attempt in June 1999 at the Little Rock National Airport in Little Rock, Arkansas. The McDonnell Douglas MD-82 aircraft overran the runway resulting in destruction of the aircraft. The Captain and 10 passengers were fatally injured.

In addition to attempting to land in spite of evidence indicating exceedance of aircraft operating manual (AOM) crosswind limitations, the aircraft was not in the correct landing configuration (i.e. spoilers were not armed), as required for a stabilized approach. The spoilers are normally armed to automatically deploy upon touchdown, reducing lift/increasing drag and assisting in aircraft deceleration. The spoilers were particularly important on this flight as the runway was wet and the increased drag could have assisted in the prevention of hydroplaning (i.e. tires losing contact with the runway surface, on a thin layer of water). Because the spoilers were not armed, upon touchdown they did not automatically deploy, or extend, resulting in excessive rollout speeds and hydroplaning, which contributed to the aircraft being unable to stop prior to overrunning the runway (NTSB, 2001).

The NTSB (2001) noted that when the AA 1420 accident occurred in 1999, the only written guidance available to the crew concerning the stabilized approach concept was a vaguely worded description of a *landing technique* in the carriers' SOPs. The NTSB (2001) stated that:

> *The only stabilized approach guidance provided in aircrew training at AA stipulated that the minimum recommended stabilized approach altitudes for IFR and visual flight rules (VFR) conditions were 1,000 and 500 feet, respectively, and that landing flaps were to be selected by 1,000 feet above ground level. Before descending below the specified minimum stabilized approach altitude, the airplane was to be in the final landing configuration (gear down and final flaps), on approach speed, on the proper flightpath, at the proper sink rate, and at stabilized thrust; these conditions were expected to be maintained throughout the rest of the approach. However, the guidance did not define what was meant by "on" approach speed, "on" the proper flightpath, and "at" the proper sink rate. In addition, the guidance did not describe the necessary flight crew actions if the stabilized approach criteria were not met. Information presented in the "Techniques" section was not considered by American to be required procedures but rather suggested ways of accomplishing a task. (p.160)*

The FAA responded to the recommendations by the NTSB with the development of the *stabilized approach concept*. The fundamental premise of the stabilized approach concept was that a general description of the aircraft state in the final approach and landing phases of flight should be based on three main aspects: (a) aircraft position on glide path and lateral extended runway centerline, (b) energy state, and (c) landing configuration (FAA, 2003). More restrictive criteria were left to the discretion of the operator and with the approval of each operator's FAA Principal Operations Inspector (POI). The POI is tasked with ensuring air carrier compliance with their FAA approved Operator SOPs.

Campbell, Schroeder, Shah, and Zaal (2018) provided additional information regarding the collaboration between the FAA, NASA, and the NTSB on unstable approaches and pilot rejected landing ADM. The researchers detailed NTSB assertions that AC 91-79A did not provide specific guidance on rejected landing requirements as recommended, which resulted in the NTSB closing the recommendation in 2012 with an unsatisfactory response. Campbell et al. (2018) contended that previous studies had not accurately investigated the root causes of the lack of compliance regarding rejected landings following an unstable approach. The researchers insisted that stable approach criteria were too complex and restrictive to the operational environment (Campbell et al., 2018).

In 2000, the FAA developed the first advisory circular on standard operating procedures (SOPs), now universally recognized as a basic component in an organization's safety management system (SMS) (FAA, 2003). An organization's SOPs are the foundation to effective crew performance and help pilots maintain an accurate mental model of an aviation task. The FAA has provided air carriers with guidance that a rejected landing is a successful outcome when given evidence of an unstable approach (FAA, 2014). Analysis of FDR data in air carriers shows that the frequency of unstable approaches was 4% in 2009. Additionally, line operations safety audit (LOSA) jump seat observers on the flight decks of 4532 commercial flights between 2002 and 2006 reported, based on visual observation of flight instrument indications, that 5% of approaches were unstable and of those only 4% of unstable approaches resulted in a rejected landing (Moriarty & Jarvis, 2014).

The Flight Safety Foundation (2009) concluded that the number of rejected landings greatly underestimates the number of unstable approaches. This evidence was based on data gathered not only by the FSF but also by the collaborative industry based Commercial Aviation Safety Team, formed by the FAA in 2008 to address runway safety (FAA, 2008). Conclusions made by both the FAA and the FSF suggest that current risk mitigation strategies have fallen short of stated objectives by the NTSB and FAA in their collaboration on the Runway Safety Council (RSC) (FSF, 2009). One of the main objectives of the RSC was to reduce the risk of REs (FAA, 2014). Although aeronautical decision making, human error, and situation awareness have been well represented in the literature, little work has been presented regarding the use of machine learning to predict probability of pilot misperception of the runway excursion hazard, when faced with evidence of an unstable approach.

Regulatory Guidance for Stabilized Approaches

The FAA has asserted that stabilized approaches are one of the most important factors in safe landings. One of the products that resulted from a working group study by the Commercial Aviation Safety Team was the creation of FAA Advisory Circular (AC) 120-71A: *Standard Operating Procedures for Flight Deck Crewmembers* (2003). In this AC, the FAA describes a stabilized approach as one in which all landing checklists and approach procedures have been completed, the aircraft is in landing configuration, on constant rate of descent, with the engines providing stable thrust, and in a position to make a normal landing on the runway in use. Appendix 2 of the AC provides other specific details of a stabilized approach:

- Flight should be stabilized by 1000' Height Above Touchdown (HAT) in Instrument Meteorological Conditions (IMC) and by 500' HAT in Visual

Meteorological Conditions (VMC).
- The airplane is on the correct track.
- The airplane is in the proper landing configuration (i.e. landing gear, flaps and slats, and speed brakes).
- After glide path intercept, the pilot flying requires no more than normal bracketing corrections to maintain the correct track and desired profile (3° descent angle, nominal) to landing within the touchdown zone.
- The airplane speed is within the acceptable range specified in the approved operating manual used by the pilot (e.g. Vref).
- The rate of descent is no greater than 1000 feet per minute (fpm).
- If an expected rate of descent greater than 1000 fpm is planned, a special approach briefing should be performed.
- Power setting is appropriate for the landing configuration selected and is within the permissible power range for approach specified in the approved operating manual used by the pilot (p. A2.1)

The FAA (2003) allows for nominal bracketing adjustments related to engine thrust, descent rate and angle of bank. Recommended ranges allow for more restrictive limitations, but are provided as follows:

- Angle of bank less than 30°
- Descent rate ± 300 fpm from target
- Operator specified thrust management, per flight manual
- Momentary exceedances are acceptable, but continuous exceedance is not considered acceptable (p. A2.2).

In the aftermath of the accident involving American Airlines Flight 1420 on June 1, 1999, the NTSB (2001) recommended that the FAA further define stabilized approach criteria. In response to the NTSB recommendations, the FAA provided a brief summarization of FAA stabilized approach oversight efforts. The FAA asserted that approach gates could be customized by a carrier as milestone points in which flight crew are to assess performance criteria during an approach, in order to maintain situation awareness concerning stabilized approach indications. These approach gates are predetermined intervals at which the flight crew compare aircraft glidepath, lateral track, and airspeed data against stabilized approach criteria. It is at these intervals where the flight crew must use the information determined from the stabilized approach criteria to make the decision to either continue the approach to landing or to execute a rejected landing (NTSB, 2001).

The FAA assigns a Principal Operations Inspector (POI) to provide regulatory oversight and guidance to each air carrier. Among other functions, the POI applies federal oversight to the carrier on the stabilized approach concept stated in FAA Order 8900.1 (2007) as follows:

- Airspeed within 5 knots of approach speed at the 100-foot decision height (DH),
- The flight deck remains within the lateral confines of the runway at the 100-foot DH,
- After passing the outer marker (OM), the glidepath deviation does not exceed one half of full deflection, and
- After passing the middle marker (MM), no unusual changes in aircraft occur. (p. 4-221)

Turbojet aircraft operators must incorporate procedures that are based on stabilized approach criteria set forth in FAA Order 8900.1, as well as the recommended guidelines provided in FAA AC 120-71A (subsequently AC 91-79A). Additionally, operator standard operating procedures (SOPs) may incorporate more restrictive stabilized approach criteria than that provided by FAA guidance from these two documents. Each carrier must provide flight crew training and SOP materials which contain a description of acceptable deviations from glidepath and lateral track when covering approach and landing procedures. Once the operator's training programs are approved by the FAA, the carrier is not free to revise these procedures without approval from their POI.

The purpose of the approach gate criterion is to provide the flight crew with target values to fly, as displayed on flight deck instruments (to assess the feasibility and safety of continuing the approach to landing or to execute a rejected landing). In its report on AA Flight 1420, the NTSB notes that the pilots should have executed a rejected landing during the final approach, when stabilized approach criteria were not met. The failure of the flight crew to configure the landing flap configuration before reaching 1,000 feet AGL, and their failure to maintain a normal rate of descent, combined with deteriorating weather conditions, decreased the safety margin enough that the pilots should have executed a rejected landing (NTSB, 2001).

Unstable approaches and runway excursions. The NTSB (2013) presents additional details on the importance of ADM in the rejected landing process in its report on the accident involving an Embraer 505 regional jet. The NTSB listed the primary contributory cause of the accident as failure of the pilots to execute a rejected landing when faced with evidence of an unstable approach. The correct approach reference speed was 110 knots indicated airspeed (KIAS), and the FDR data indicated that an actual approach speed of 158 KIAS was flown. The approach speed exceedance contributed to a RE as the aircraft experienced a runway overrun, resulting in destruction of the aircraft. Runway excursion caused by unstable approach landing was stated as the primary contributory factor in this accident, as well as approximately 10 other accidents and incidents per year from 2005 to 2016 resulting in the NTSB issuing Safety Recommendations

A-08-16 through A-08-20 (FAA, 2014a, 2014b; NTSB, 2016). These Safety Recommendations detailed significant deficiencies in industry-based initiatives mitigating the risk of runway excursions with pilot training substantiated with evidence presented in NASA ASRS pilot reports (NTSB, 2008).

Several recent examples of accidents with UARM-like contributory factors are described by the NTSB:

- Pakistan International Airlines Flight 8303 crashed while on approach to Jinnah International Airport in Karachi, Pakistan. The A320 exceeded stable approach criteria (airspeed, descent rate, configuration, and glideslope deviation) resulting in fatal injuries to 97 of the 99 souls on board (AAIB, 2020).
- Asiana Air Flight 214 crashed at the San Francisco International Airport, due to a RE caused by exceedance of glidepath stabilized approach criteria. The accident resulted in destruction of the Boeing 777 as well as fatal injuries to three passengers (NTSB, 2014).
- UPS Flight 1354 crashed while attempting an approach to landing at the Birmingham-Shuttlesworth International Airport, Birmingham, Alabama in August 2013. The NTSB lists the primary cause of the accident as the flight crew continuing an unstable approach to landing, resulting in destruction of the Airbus A300 as well as fatally injuring the sole occupants, the two pilots. The NTSB reports that the A300 exceeded stable approach criteria based on incorrect landing configuration and excessive glidepath deviations, resulting in the aircraft impacting the ground short of the runway (NTSB, 2014).
- Federal Express (FedEx) Flight 14 crashed during landing at the Newark International Airport, Newark, New Jersey in July 1997, resulting in destruction of the

McDonnell Douglas MD-11. The NTSB states that the probable cause of the accident was the Captain's lapse in ADM, continuing a landing with evidence of exceedance of stabilized approach criteria (i.e. excessive descent rate). The unstable approach resulted in a hard landing, bounce, loss of control, and ultimately a RE (NTSB, 2000).

These examples of lapses in aeronautical decision making, which result in the occurrence of UARM and REs, provide evidence of an aviation hazard. Large amounts of flight operations data have been collected with the advent of Flight Data Monitoring technologies. The evolution of advanced and complex data processing algorithms has provided aviation researchers with the opportunity to explore what patterns or relationships might exist in these large flight data.

Pilot risk perception and risk tolerance. A key point in the study is the prediction of pilot risk misperception. The FAA (1991) relates pilot risk management to task accomplishment in AC 60-22, Aeronautical Decision Making, with the self-assessment technique of asking oneself, "Is the success of the task worth the risk?" (p. 22). Orasanu et al. (2001) describe a relative lack of aviation research on pilot risk perception and risk tolerance. The researchers continue to describe the importance of better understanding of pilot risk perception and risk tolerance in the ADM process. Martinussen and Hunter (2010) assert that pilot risk assessment and management are crucial aspects of pilot ADM. They then define pilot risk perception as "recognition of the risk inherent in a situation" (p. 198). Hunter (2005) professes that pilots can be prone to display poor risk judgement and substantially underestimate risk. The researcher's conclusions are based on evidence of pilots pressing on when faced with evidence of deteriorating performance conditions, while underestimating the impact of external factors to the aircraft and overestimating their self-capacity to accomplish certain tasks. The conclusions of Hunter (2005) are in agreement with those reached by both Orasansu et al. (2001) and Dismukes (2010) regarding the propensity of pilots to exhibit lapses in ADM regarding continuation bias (i.e., pressing on or continuation errors). Hunter (2005) states that risk perception can be mediated by both pilot self-assessment, as well as more accurate mental modeling of the environment. Martinussen and Hunter (2010) conclude that risk perception is primarily a cognitive activity and involves the accurate perception and projection of aircraft state and external factors, and the resulting mental model, to maintain a high level of situation awareness.

Hunter (2005) provides further evidence of pilot risk perception measurement using a Hazardous Attitude Scale (HAS). Airline pilots were presented with 10 different aviation scenarios and provided alternative solutions to assess ADM. Hunter concludes that poor risk perception was a more significant variable than poor risk tolerance. For example, pilots who experienced significantly more hazardous events generally rated hazardous scenarios less risky than those pilots who had experienced fewer hazardous events. Hunter subsequently deduces that poor correlation between pilot hazardous experiences and estimation of risk supports this supposition.

Hunter (2005) further expands the definition of pilot risk perception as the cognitive ability of the pilot to appraise and discern risk, while involved in the process of formulating an environmental mental model. The researcher goes on to describe the misconception of risk perception when this appraisal of a situation is in error. When the pilot either underestimates the risk inherent in the situation or overestimates his/her own capabilities, pilot risk perception error is probable.

You and Han (2013) discuss the effects of risk perception and flight experience on airline pilot attitudes relative to safety operational behaviors. They also state that pilot risk perception is a crucial pilot attribute regarding hazards. Their research affirms their supposition that pilot risk perception enables pilots to mitigate risk, while addressing the cognitive demands inherent to flight operations.

Benbassat and Abramson (2002) provide research on pilot landing risk perception with their study on landing accidents and pilot risk perception. The researchers analyzed over 6,000 NTSB accident reports whose contributory factors included runway excursions. The researchers also surveyed student and GA pilots on their perceptions of risk in the landing flare maneuver. Their findings corroborate those of Hunter (2005) regarding pilot underestimation of risk inherent in landings. The researchers recommend further research involving pilot perception of risk in the approach and landing phases of flight.

Ju, Ji, Lan, and You (2017) describe how narcissistic personality issues factor into risk perception and how overoptimistic expectations affect pilot perception of risk in Chinese pilots. Recommendations based on their findings include the necessity for pilots to accurately compare risk estimates with actual risk. They further describe the challenges inherent in the measurement and assessment of aviation risk. However, they assert that the measurement of pilot risk perception is less difficult and can be determined based on optimism bias to reflect risk estimation. Thus, while their study focused on optimism bias, they recommend further research on other cognitive biases which could significantly affect accuracy of risk perception. IATA (2017) corroborates results of the study with the assertion that pilots may sometimes continue an unstable approach to landing due to factors such as peer pressure, organizational pressure to meet schedule, and perceptions of company policy regarding rejected landing decision making. IATA also suggests that pilot perception risk associated with the rejected landing maneuver is higher than continuing an unstable approach to landing.

Campbell, Schroeder, Shah, and Zaal (2018) conducted experimental research at the NASA Ames Research Center on perceptions of pilot risk concerning unstable approach recovery to landing and risk perception of various unstable approach conditions. Research was conducted using 36 professional airline pilot subjects and three full motion Level-D flight simulators: B747, B737, and A330. Level D flight simulators were the highest rated of four ratings (A through D) and provided full motion feedback to the pilots by means of a motion platform. Level D simulators also provided accurate flight control feedback to pilots and simulated other aircraft systems including avionics and advanced electronic flight instrument systems (EFIS). The FAA provided certification approval guidance to air carriers in AC 61-136A, *FAA Approval of Aviation Training Devices and Their Use for Training and Experience* (FAA, 2014b). The researchers utilized an experimental design that removed the rejected landing decision-making process in order to assess landing performance under various unstable approach conditions. The stated objective of the research was to determine if more effective rejected landing criteria were possible. One ancillary purpose of this research was to investigate pilot landing performance under various approach states to determine which limitations were most critical in pilot landings. Results indicated that energy state management parameters associated with excessive approach speeds and descent rate were the most important predictors in pilot landing performance. Although not listed in experimental controls, energy state management associated with engine power settings was observed to be an important predictor of landing performance and was recommended by the researchers to be more closely scrutinized in future research (Campbell, Schroeder, Shah & Zaal, 2018).

Boeing Commercial Airplanes (BCA) (2017) has compiled data on commercial aircraft accidents worldwide since 1959. Boeing reported that the highest percentage of fatal accidents over the last 10 years occurred during the approach and landing phases of flight as shown in Figure 1. Boeing also emphasized the contrast of relatively low flight time in the approach and landing phases of flight and the higher percentage of fatal accidents relative to other phases of flight (BCA, 2017).

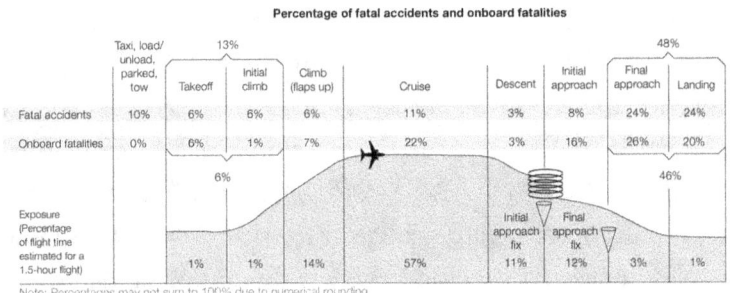

Figure 1. Fatal accidents and onboard fatalities by phase of flight from 2007–2016. Percentages may not sum to 100% due to numerical rounding. Reprinted from "Statistical Summary of Commercial Jet Airplane Accidents Worldwide Operations: 1959-2016," Aviation Safety, 2017. Copyright 2017 by Boeing Commercial Airplanes, p. 20. Adapted with permission. Source: www.skybrary.aero

To facilitate safety risk mitigation strategies for commercial airline operators, the FAA commissioned a working group, the Commercial Aviation Safety Team (CAST), in 2002. One of the key recommendations from the CAST was the drafting of Advisory Circular (AC) 120-71A, *Standard Operating Procedures for Flight Deck Crewmembers* (subsequently replaced with AC 120-71B). This Advisory Circular introduced stabilized approach criteria, based on aircraft glide path, energy state, and configuration for landing (FAA, 2003). The FAA subsequently removed the stabilized approach criteria from AC 120-71A when it was updated to AC-120-71B. Although the specific criteria for the stabilized approach concept was not listed subsequent documentation, the FAA provided guidance on stable approaches in AC-91-79A, *Mitigating the Risks of a Runway Overrun Upon Landing*. In this AC, the FAA presented a case study on an unstable approach scenario as well as listing unstabilized approaches as the primary contributory factor in runway excursions (FAA, 2009, p. 3). Although FAA stable approach criteria have not been updated or modified in subsequent advisory circulars, both AC-120-71A and AC-91-79A have been referred to in FAA documentation regarding unstable approaches. For example, the FAA advised readers to "refer to AC-120-71" in its description of stabilized approaches in AC-120-108, *Continuous Descent Final Approach*, (FAA, 2011, p. 2) and also made a similar suggestion in FAA Safety Briefing 18-09, *FAA Stabilized Approach and Go-Around Concept*, but referred readers instead to AC-91-79A (FAA, 2018, p. 2). References to specific FAA stable approach criteria were made to those listed in AC-120-71A (FAA, 2003) in this research.

The FAA also discussed unstable approaches in recommendations made to pilots concerning energy state management techniques in Advisory Circular 120-111, *Upset Recovery and Prevention Training*. In this AC, the FAA asserted that proper energy state management was a critical component in flight path management associated with stable approaches. (FAA, 2017a). Figure 2 shows an overview of a stabilized approach.

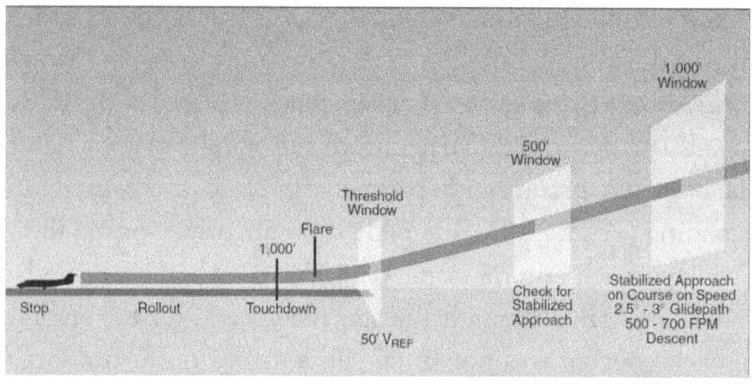

Figure 2. Stabilized approach. Reprinted from "Air Traffic Bulletin Procedures (ATB 2019-1)," by Federal Aviation Administration Air Traffic Procedures, April 2019, p. 2. Retrieved from https://www.faa.gov/air_traffic/publications/media/atb_april_2019.pdf

Additionally, in Advisory Circular 91-79A the FAA informed operators of the importance of safety risk mitigation strategies regarding runway excursions and highlighted concerns associated with unstable approaches. The FAA asserted that exceedances in stable approach criteria could be contributory factors in runway excursions (FAA, 2013). For example, approach airspeed exceedance could cause a long landing, contributing to a runway overrun.

In 2008, the FAA formed the Runway Safety Council in collaboration with industry, to address hazards associated with runway safety. One of the stated goals of this cooperative effort was to decrease the number and severity of REs (FAA, 2008). The FAA asserted that REs play a crucial role in the overall risk-based scope of runway safety, with over 30 percent of REs resulting in accidents (FAA, 2008). The FAA and industry stakeholders subsequently developed action plans to reduce REs focused on identifying important factors that contribute to REs, using a data-driven approach (FAA, 2015).

An NTSB (2013) report presented details on the importance of aeronautical decision making (ADM) in the unstable approach/rejected landing process in an accident involving an Embraer 505 (also known as the Embraer Phenom 300 light jet) regional jet. The primary contributory cause of the accident was the failure of the pilots to execute a rejected landing when faced with evidence of an unstable approach (NTSB, 2013). The NTSB noted that the correct approach reference speed was 110 knots indicated airspeed (KIAS); however, data from the flight data recorder (FDR) indicated an actual approach speed of 158 KIAS. The approach speed exceedance contributed to a RE as the aircraft experienced a runway overrun, resulting in destruction of the aircraft.

RESEARCH OVERVIEW

Runway excursion caused by unstable approach to a landing was stated as the primary contributory factor in an average of 10 accidents and incidents per year from 2005 to 2016, resulting in the NTSB issuing Safety Recommendations A-08-16 through A-08-20 (FAA, 2014a, 2014b; NTSB, 2016). These Safety Recommendations detailed significant deficiencies in industry-based initiatives mitigating the risk of runway excursions through pilot training alone, substantiated with evidence presented in NASA Aviation Safety Reporting System (ASRS) pilot reports (NTSB, 2008). The suggested lapse in ADM, which occurs when a pilot elects to continue an unstable approach to landing, thus risking a runway excursion, was defined as Unstable Approach Risk Misperception (UARM) in the research.

Several examples of accidents with UARM-like contributory factors have been reported by the NTSB:

- Asiana Air Flight 214 crashed at the San Francisco International Airport, due to a RE (veer-off) caused by exceedance of glidepath stabilized approach criteria (well below glidepath). The accident resulted in destruction of the Boeing 777 as well as fatal injuries to three passengers (NTSB, 2014).
- UPS Flight 1354 crashed while attempting a night instrument approach to a landing at the Birmingham-Shuttlesworth International Airport, Birmingham, Alabama in August 2013. The NTSB reported the

primary cause of the accident was the flight crew continuing an unstable approach to landing, resulting in destruction of the Airbus A300 as well as fatally injuring the sole occupants, the two pilots. The report noted that the A300 exceeded stable approach criteria based on excessive glidepath deviations (below glidepath), resulting in the aircraft impacting the ground short of the runway (NTSB, 2014).
- Federal Express (FedEx) Flight 14 crashed during landing at the Newark International Airport, Newark, New Jersey in July 1997, resulting in destruction of the McDonnell Douglas MD-11. The NTSB stated that the probable cause of the accident was the Captain's lapse in ADM, continuing a landing with evidence of exceedance of stabilized approach criteria (excessive descent rate). The unstable approach resulted in a hard, bounced landing, leading to a loss of directional control on the runway, and ultimately a RE (NTSB, 2000).

Based on these and other related aviation accidents and incidents associated with REs, the NTSB (2019b) issued Safety Alert 077 advising pilots that failure to reject a landing associated with an unstable approach could result in not only an RE, but also loss of control and/or collision with terrain. In this Safety Alert, the NTSB advised pilots who face evidence of an unstable approach at 500 ft in visual conditions, to execute a rejected landing. The NTSB also advised pilots to beware of operational pressures and continuation bias to continue a landing attempt when unstable, and reiterated the importance of performing a rejected landing when faced with evidence of an unstable approach (NTSB, 2019b).

These examples of lapses in ADM, which resulted in the occurrence of UARM and REs, provide evidence of an aviation hazard. The FAA explained the importance of ADM as it related to pilot risk management in AC 60-22, *Aeronautical Decision*

Making. In this document, the FAA detailed how pilot risk mismanagement could lead to aviation incidents and accidents (FAA, 1991). Orasansu et al. (2001) provided details on the criticality of risk perception in ADM with a discussion of several perspectives on risk perception factors such as: (a) organizational pressures, (b) pilot experience levels, (c) job responsibilities, and (d) mental modeling. The researchers described pilot risk tolerance and perception as they relate to ADM as depicted in Figure 3.

Figure 3. Risk management decision-making process. From "Pilot's Handbook of Aeronautical Knowledge (FAA-H-8083-25)," by Federal Aviation Administration, 2016 (https://www.faa.gov/regulations_policies/handbooks_manuals/aviation/phak/media/04_phak_ch2.pdf). In the public domain.

Additionally, the FAA (2016) asserted that the goal of risk management "is to proactively identify safety-related hazards and mitigate the associated risks" (p. 2-3). The FAA continued to describe how the development of good risk assessment skills were necessary for pilots to demonstrate successful ADM.

Hunter (2005) provided much of the foundational research on pilot risk perception of hazards. Hunter defined pilot risk perception as the cognitive ability to appraise and discern risk involved in the formulation of an environmental mental model. The researcher detailed the misconception of risk perception when this appraisal of a situation is in error. When pilots either underestimate the risk inherent in the situation or overestimate their own capabilities, pilot risk perception error is probable. You and Han (2013) build on the work of Hunter (2005) with the assertion that the effects of airline pilot risk perception on threat and error management (TEM) are significant. Effective risk perception aspects of ADM enable pilots to successfully identify hazards while addressing the cognitive demands inherent to flight operations.

Orasanu et al. (2001) described how inappropriate risk perception could contribute to lapses in ADM. The researchers described how *continuation errors*, also referred to as *continuation bias* by Dismukes (2010), could occur when pilot ADM and SA do not evolve and adapt to a dynamic environment. For example, if evidence of an unstable approach becomes apparent to the flight crew and they elect to continue to landing, as originally planned, Dismukes (2010) and Orasanu et al. (2001) assert that *continuation bias* may have been experienced.

Pilots have been trained to compare actual aircraft performance variables, such as (a) indicated airspeed, (b) descent rate, (c) angle of bank, and (d) engine thrust, with stable approach criteria recommended by the FAA and further customized by each operator. Based on this assessment, pilots are expected to execute a rejected landing if stable approach criteria have not been met (Moriarty & Jarvis, 2014). Although the literature indicated that several variations of the term *rejected landing* have been used interchangeably (i.e., missed approach or go-around), for purposes of standardization, the term *rejected landing* was used in this research when referring to the procedure pilots perform to abandon a landing attempt.

Although pilots have been trained to reject landings based on evidence of an unstable approach, a study by Giles (2013) on compliance with Standard Operating Procedures (SOP), an aspect of Aeronautical Decision Making, stated the following:

> *For the most part pilots will comply with SOP, but when they (1) don't agree with SOP, (2) don't understand SOP or the risks associated with not complying with SOP, or (3) don't feel adequately trained to know what SOP is, it is difficult to motivate them to comply. (p.2)*

Hence, pilots may not comply with stabilized approach criteria if they do not perceive the risk of a runway excursion associated with not executing the required rejected landing. The FAA suggested that one possible consideration to this risk misperception was that 97% of unstabilized approaches have resulted in a safe landing, although 10% of these *safe landings* exceeded some parameter (e.g. landing long). Regardless, the FAA suggested that non-compliance with an SOP was indicative of ineffective ADM (FAA, 2016).

With the continued advancements in FDR and Cockpit Voice Recorder (CVR) technology on commercial airliners, large volumes of data have been recorded and archived at a very rapid pace (Walker, 2017). W. Vogt, G. Vogt, Gardner, and Haeffele (2014) define *big data* as data so large in volume that it would be impossible for one person to code and analyze in less than one year without utilizing a computer. FDR technology was originally used to assist accident investigations with mathematical analytical techniques concurrently evolving as FDR technology improved. As a result of these developments, new applications in safety risk management (SRM) emerged. Examples of these SRM processes include the Flight Operations Quality Assurance (FOQA) and FDM programs (Treder & Crane, 2004).

The advent of large data gathering methods has also provided the impetus for the continued development of advanced data analytical tools. Other industries have utilized advanced techniques in computing capability to develop complex mathematical algorithms with the capability to handle large data (Tufféry, 2011). Recently, aviation researchers have begun to utilize these advanced data analytical tools in the exploration of large flight data (Li, Das, Hansman, Palacios, & Srivastava, 2015). Machine learning (ML) techniques have emerged as a preferred technique to rapidly analyze large volumes of flight data (Koteeswaran, Malarvizhi, Kannan, Sasikala, & Geetha, 2017).

The purpose of the research was to utilize machine learning techniques to explore large flight data in order to predict UARM. The exploration focused on the approach and landing phases of flight, specifically on unstable approaches. Variable selection processes were based on the stable approach criteria as defined in AC 120-71A (FAA, 2003) and AC-91-79A (FAA, 2014). Variables were defined using the recorded flight data parameters including: (a) target approach speed deviation, (b) flap position, (c) landing gear position, (d) engine speed, and (e) glide path deviation. Additional criteria were based on: (a) vertical and lateral position of the aircraft with reference to the landing runway, (b) energy state, and (c) landing configuration.

The information gathered in the data analysis was used to predict the probability of the pilot misperceiving the runway excursion risk of continuing an unstable approach to landing. Pilot misperception was represented by non-compliance (either intentional or not) with standard operating procedures regarding FAA guidance on required actions when faced with evidence of an unstabilized approach. Machine learning techniques were used to populate and compare various predictive models, and to determine the most accurate model, which was then used to make predictions of the probability of the manifestation of the target dependent variable, UARM. The occurrence of UARM contradicts best safety practices as recommended by the NTSB and the guidance by the FAA, which is considered the minimum requirement in the operations specifications (OPSPECS) of any air carrier (FAA, 2003, 2014; NTSB, 2016, 2019b).

Identifying the Aviation Problem

Runway excursions are an aviation safety risk associated with hazards inherent in unstable approaches. The NTSB described problems of continuing unstable approach to landing in Safety Alert 077 (2019b). In this document, the NTSB (2019b) listed problems associated with unstable approaches as:

- Failure to establish and maintain a stabilized approach, or continuing an unstabilized approach, could lead to landing too fast or too far down the runway, potentially resulting in a runway excursion, loss of control, or collision with terrain.
- Regardless of the type of aircraft, the level of pilot experience, or whether the flight was being conducted under instrument flight rules or visual flight rules, an unstabilized approach was a key contributor to runway excursions, loss of control, and terrain collisions control. (p. 1)

The FAA and NTSB have consistently identified unstable approaches as one of the most frequent causal factors in aircraft runway excursions, with flight data indicating an average of 10 accidents per year from 2005 to 2016 (FAA, 2014, 2016; NTSB, 2010, 2016). The FSF (2009) presented details concerning the hazards associated with unstable approaches and the risk of runway excursion that resulted when pilots elected to continue to landing. The FAA, NASA, and the NTSB have confirmed the existence of the hazard and have made efforts to address the issue with guidance to air carriers regarding the following: (a) aircrew training, (b) SOP enhancement, and (c) safety mitigation strategies (e.g. pilot simulator training scenarios). However, an analysis of flight data gathered via LOSA, FOQA, and NASA ASRS voluntary pilot reports revealed that this hazard continued to exist (FAA, 2003, 2014; FSF, 2009; NTSB, 2014a, 2014b, 2016, 2019b). The NTSB has communicated its concern that even though air carriers now have stabilized approach guidance, as described in FAA Flight Standards HBAT 98-22, runway excursions have continued to occur in part due to lapses in pilot perception of the risk when faced with evidence of an unstable approach (FSF, 2009; NTSB, 2001, 2016, 2019b).

Purpose of the Research

The purpose of this research was to utilize machine learning techniques to explore large flight data in order to predict UARM. The study had two main objectives: (a) use machine learning algorithms to develop a prediction model for UARM, and (b) determine variables that contribute to the prediction of UARM. Predictive models were constructed based on advanced machine learning algorithms using 186 recorded flight data variables. Specific machine learning techniques applied to the flight data included: (a) decision tree, (b) logistic regression, (c) neural network, (d) support vector machine, (e) random forest, and (f) gradient boost machine algorithms.

The flight data were recorded by FDRs on a fleet of 35 regional jets over a period of four years (2001-2004). NASA had de-identified these data and made them available to the public. These data points were analyzed to identify unstable approaches and to construct prediction models. Once the models were built and validated, the model with the highest predictive score was used to predict the probability of UARM, which could be used to identify RE hazard. Additionally, SAS™ EM® software was used to rank flight data variables in order of importance to the occurrence of UARM. SAS™ EM® defined variable worth as the rank order (from 0 to 1) of input variables determined by the

Chi-square statistic and described the strength of the relationship between categorical input variables and the target variable. SAS™ EM® used *binning* to derive categorical input variables from continuous input variables (Sarma, 2013).

Significance of the Study

The research helps to enhance the effectiveness of commercial airline pilot simulator training as a hazard mitigation strategy by utilizing scenarios involving unstable approaches. Given the ability to predict UARM and the identification of flight variables most important in the prediction of UARM, airline training managers can evaluate and improve pilot ADM specifically to mitigate runway excursions.

The development of prediction models based on the application of ML algorithms to recorded flight data was a seminal study that focused on using data mining of data to build models to predict a desired or undesired event. Additionally, the results of predictive algorithms could be used to detect lapses in decision making in other high risk fields such as medicine (e.g., surgery). For example, medical professionals perform many of the similar tasks requiring decisions to be made based on safety of the patient. This decision-making ability relies on the management of risk and the perception of risk versus an estimate of one's ability to complete the task; the predictive algorithm could provide the capability to the medical professional to mitigate and reduce such risk The ability to predetermine exceedance could also contribute to the evolution of pilot alerting technologies, such as Honeywell's SmartLanding™ software algorithms that increase pilot SA of the aircraft state in the approach and landing phases of flight.

Key beneficiaries of the research are airline pilot simulator training programs and airline Safety Management System managers. The ability of airline pilot training managers to not only predict UARM but also identify hazardous trends in aircraft state variables involved in ADM could have a positive impact on airline safety risk mitigation strategies inherent in pilot simulator training programs, such as developing realistic runway excursion scenarios. Results of the study could be used to further refine not only FAA (2014) stabilized approach criteria but also in the oversight of air carrier pilot training programs.

Safety Management Systems managers could use the results of the study to improve SRM effectiveness, as required under 14CFR Part 5. Because SMS programs have traditionally relied on hazard identification using accident and incident reports rather than proactive measures, predictive capabilities could be beneficial. The ability to predict UARM could provide SMS managers with a predictive tool that would enhance safety risk mitigation effectiveness.

Research Questions

The study was exploratory and data-driven in nature, based on the following research questions (RQ):

- RQ 1: How can the application of data-mining and machine learning techniques to recorded flight data be used to predict the probability of *Unstable Approach Risk Misperception* by the pilot?
- RQ 2: What flight data variables are the most important predictors of pilot misperception of a runway excursion hazard as evidenced by continuing an unstable approach to a landing?

Delimitations

Exceedance criteria described in FAA AC 120-71A were considered the threshold for determining an unstable approach. Reference approach speed criteria excluded Category A approach speeds (i.e. ≤ 90 knots), as that category generally applies to helicopters (no stall speed) and light GA airplanes certified under 14 CFR §23.49 (FAA, 2012).

Limitations and Assumptions

Limitations. The data were limited to the 186 flight variables provided by the NASA public access website for four years (2001-2004) of flight operations by 35 regional jet aircraft. No data were available regarding passenger configuration, which is used by the FAA to describe regional jet commercial aircraft (less than 100 passengers) (FAA, 2005). Because CVR data were not available for the study, CRM influence on pilot misperception could not be analyzed. Additionally, pilot/automation interface was also not available. Because only FDR aircraft state data were available, the study could not consider any other variables that may have contributed to pilot UARM, such as weather (e.g., turbulence, wind shear, cross-winds), emergency or abnormal conditions (e.g. low fuel, engine or flight control anomalies), runway conditions (e.g. contamination with snow, water, lights) or visual illusions. In addition to weather considerations, day/night flight conditions were not provided and as such, were not considered in the analysis. No data were available to indicate if any of the approaches resulted in an actual runway excursion.

Assumptions. The 186 flight data variables were sufficient to develop predictive models. The data were redacted for any identifying information such as specific air carrier, aircraft type, airports, and name/type of instrument approach, hence assumptions pertaining to certain approach parameters such as approach speed, glideslope and landing configuration were made. Because FAA guidelines have allowed for more restrictive criteria to be developed by an air carrier, it was assumed that the air carrier had an SOP that followed the FAA stable approach guidance at least as restrictive as those criteria defined in AC 120-71A. Although there was no regulatory definition of regional jets, the FAA used a passenger configuration of less than 100 passengers to describe RJs in AC 150/525-4b, *Runway Length Requirements for Airport Design* (FAA, 2005). It was assumed that the flight data were sampled from RJs configured for less than 100 passengers.

Approaches were assumed to be conducted on a three-degree glideslope, and any flap setting greater than zero was assumed to be a proper landing configuration. Pilot indications of stabilized approach criteria were assumed to be provided with standard transport aircraft flight instruments. For example, descent rate, airspeed, and glidepath indications were assumed to be provided to the pilots on industry standard pilot display technology, such as electronic flight instrument systems (EFIS), primary flight display (PFD) and navigational display (ND) avionics. Target reference approach speed range was assumed to be from 105 to 140 knots indicated airspeed and was based on FAA approach category airspeed determination characteristics detailed in Title 14 CFR, Chapter I, Subchapter F, Part 97, Subpart A., § 97.3 (FAA, 2012). Additionally, target approach speed was assumed to be calculated based on a zero-wind condition. Pilots flying the aircraft represented in the study were fully qualified professional pilots.

Summary

The FAA and NTSB have identified unstable approaches as one of the primary contributory factors to runway excursion hazards (FAA, 2014; NTSB, 2000, 2001, 2014, 2014, 2016, 2019b). In the effort to enhance runway safety, the FAA has stipulated that operators adhere to criteria defining stable approaches (FAA, 2003, 2014). Data indicated that although unstable approaches still occurred, pilots may not have always followed the FAA guidance by performing a rejected landing (FAA, 2014; FSF, 2009).

Non-compliance, whether intentional or not, of FAA approved air carrier OPSPECS and SOPs concerning stabilized approaches, suggested a lapse in pilot ADM, and often had been included as a primary contributory factor in accidents and incidents involving runway excursions (NTSB, 2016, 2019b). With the advent and deployment of advanced digital data recording devices, required under 14CFR §91.609 for all air carriers with an operating certificate, opportunities exist to sample and analyze recorded flight data. Concurrently, recent developments in complex mathematical machine learning algorithms have improved research capability regarding the analysis of these flight data (Oehling & Barry, 2019). Data mining techniques, both exploratory and predictive, have provided aviation researchers the tools necessary to both analyze these large flight data and also to predict abnormal flight occurrences.

The results of the study present an example of aviation research using machine learning to predict *Unstable Approach Risk Misperception*. Subsequent chapters present a review of relevant peer-reviewed research, including gaps in the literature. Six machine learning algorithms were used for the analysis to identify which most accurately modeled the prediction of the probability of pilot misperception of runway excursion risk, as well as to identify the stabilized approach criteria flight variables associated with frequent non-compliance of rejected landing guidelines. Finally, recommendations for further research are made, based on how large flight data monitoring can be used to improve and enhance aviation safety through training, procedures, and aircraft flight instrument design.

DISCUSSION, CONCLUSIONS, AND RECOMMENDATIONS

The study addressed two areas of aviation safety: (a) pilot aeronautical decision-making lapses regarding unstable approaches and (b) the ability to predict *Unstable Approach Risk Misperception*. A new algorithm, based on UARM, was successfully developed and deployed to augment other advanced machine learning algorithms used to explore large recorded flight data. Data mining techniques were also successfully applied to recorded flight data in order to develop predictive models. Federal Aviation Administration stable approach exceedance criteria were employed to investigate unstable approaches, their impact factors, and suggested lapses in pilot aeronautical decision-making regarding landing or rejected landing. Results of the study demonstrated that large recorded flight data could be used to discover new knowledge in flight operations.

Results of the study successfully demonstrated the deployment of a new algorithm which was used as a predictive tool for UARM. The scalability of the new algorithm was employed with the adaptation, application, and comparison of six advanced machine learning algorithms to recorded flight data. The UARM algorithm was then used to predict conditions when pilots continued an unstable approach, rather than executing a rejected landing, which indicated a lapse in pilot aeronautical decision-making. Because of this evidence obtained in the demonstration, decision makers should be able to utilize this predictive capability to mitigate the hazards associated with pilot misperception of runway excursions.

Discussion

A knowledge discovery process was used to facilitate the prediction of a known aviation hazard: runway excursion caused by continuation of an unstable approach to landing. The research questions were addressed regarding the application of machine learning alorithms and predictive modeling of recorded flight data; as well as the prediction of the probability of UARM and how to identify important predictors of UARM. The study supported the findings of Oehling and Barry (2019), whose research showed that ML techniques could be applied to large recorded flight data for purposes of knowledge discovery. Another similarity in the findings of the study and that of Oehling and Barry (2019) was the observation and recommendation that the application of the knowldege discovery process should consider other phases of flight, not only the approach and landing phase.

One key difference with Oehling and Barry (2019) was the disagreement in results indicating that the NN model was among the ML techniques with the highest predictive power. Somewhat unexpected was that the Decision Tree model was the model that had the highest predictive power. The literature had indicated that advancements in ensemble learning algorithms such as Random Forest and Gradient Boost Machine should provide modeling capacities that outperform traditional ML algorithms such as Decision Tree-based models. Additionally, this finding did not support the assertion of Paul and Dupont (2015) that Random Forest should perform the best among ML techniques regarding the discovery embedded variables selected in the feature selection process.

The flight data were recorded by FDRs on a fleet of 35 regional jets over a period of four years. NASA had de-identified these data and made them available to the public. These data were analyzed to identify unstable approaches and to construct prediction models. Several factors ensured the validity of not only the AVSKD process, but also the validity of the data used in the research. At the time of the study, the FAA stable approach exceedance criteria had not been modified or changed since originally developed. The stable approach criteria listed in Appendix 2 of FAA AC 120-71A were still used in SOP guidance for Part 121 US air carriers at both the time of data collection and of the study. The scalability of the UARM algorithm allowed for the implementation of these flight data, and flight data variables were successfully identified to represent the stable approach constructs. Additionally, unstable approaches were successfully identified based on the assessment of flight data variables.

The identification and extraction of unstable approach occurrence was critical to the deployment of the UARM algorithm. Additionally, algorithm scalability ensured that no performance fallibility would be expected with the application of flight data gathered on other airframe types or models or timeframe of data collection. For example, the AVSKD and UARM algorithm process would be expected to demonstrate both reliability and validity independent on the data source (i.e., Boeing 747, Embraer 145, Airbus 320, etc.). Scalability of the UARM algorithm included the timeframe of data collection would not have been expected to affect the reliability and/or validity of the model as well. For example, results indicated that the data collected for the study did not affect model performance, hence, no effects would be expected if the opportunity for a more recent data source became available for public research.

The purpose of the research was to utilize machine learning techniques to explore large flight data in order to predict the target variable, *Unstable Approach Risk Misperception*. Machine learning algorithms were used to develop a prediction model for *Unstable Approach Risk Misperception* and to determine important variables that contributed to the prediction of *Unstable Approach Risk Misperception*. Predictive models were constructed based on advanced machine learning algorithms using 186 recorded flight data variables. Specific machine learning techniques applied to the flight data included: (a) decision tree with 2, 3 and 5 branches, (b) logistic regression, (c) neural network, (d) support vector machine, (e) random forest, and (f) gradient boost machine algorithms. Once the models were built and validated, the model with the highest predictive score was used to predict the probability of UARM, which could be used to identify runway excursion hazard. Additionally, SAS® EM™ software was used to rank flight data variables considered to be most important to the occurrence of UARM.

The research was exploratory and data-driven in nature, based on answering two research questions:

Research Question 1. How can the application of data-mining and machine learning techniques to recorded flight data be used to predict the probability of *Unstable Approach Risk Misperception* by the pilot?

The research question was addressed with the development of a new algorithm based on unstable approach identification and subsequent occurrence (or not) of UARM. Additionally, predictive models using advanced machine learning algorithms were successfully employed with the application of these models to recorded flight data. Data mining techniques were successfully used to explore a large-volume FDR data from commercial flight operations and to predict *Unstable Approach Risk Misperception*. Data coding was successfully developed using FAA stable approach exceedance criteria, which was applied to FDR flight data. A new algorithm was successfully developed using the *Aviation Safety Knowledge Discovery* model developed and validated by Mathews et al. (2013) at the NASA Ames Research Center.

Pressing On

The successful development and deployment of the UARM algorithm was a key accomplishment of the study. The UARM algorithm successfully demonstrated how large flight data could be used to predict the probability of pilot risk misperception regarding the hazard of runway excursion. Evidence of pilot risk misperception was represented by the decision of the pilot to continue to a landing even when evidence existed of exceedance in any one or more of the flight data variables from the FAA stabilized approach criteria. For purposes of this research, this target variable was defined as *Unstable Approach Risk Misperception* (UARM). Data mining techniques were used to populate and compare various predictive models and to determine the most accurate model, decision tree with three branches, which was then used to make predictions of the target variable.

In order to predict the probability that UARM would occur during an unstable approach, the following ML algorithms were used to build the models: (a) logistic regression, (b) decision tree with 2, 3, and 5 branches, (c) neural network, (d) support vector machine, (e) gradient boost machine, and (f) random forest. Results indicated flight-related variables representing: (1) glide-slope deviation, (2) selected approach speed (3) localizer deviation, (6) flaps not extended, (7) excessive drift angle, and (8) approach speed deviation were the most important predictors of probability of UARM occurrence. Additionally, the occurrence of a rejected landing, or continued approach to landing, when confronted with evidence of an unstable approach, was also included.

Findings indicated that the DT model performed with the highest predictive power, 96%. Once the DT model was determined to be the highest scoring model, a separate data set (2004 FDR data) was used to: (a) determine the predictive probability of the target variable, UARM, and (b) rank input variables in order of importance. Results of this analysis described the predictive accuracy of UARM as 98%. A sensitivity and specificity analysis was conducted which indicated a true positive prediction of 96% and a true negative prediction of 92%. Thus, the model was acceptable to answer the question of how to predict the probability of UARM.

Research Question 2. What flight data variables are the most important predictors of pilot misperception of a runway excursion hazard as evidenced by continuing an unstable approach to a landing?

The research question was successfully addressed by analyzing the recorded flight data, specifically the approach and landing phases of flight which indicated exceedance of FAA stable approach criteria, and using these criteria to develop and compare several different predictive models. The successful development and deployment of the new UARM algorithm provided an appropriate tool to accomplish this task. These data were extracted using snapshots at two assessment windows, once again using FAA stable approach assessment criteria. Data was sampled at a 500 ft AGL assessment window and also at a point of either landing or a rejected landing (WOW either greater than or equal to 0).

Assessment was conducted using the flight data variables with FAA AC-120-71A (FAA, 2003) providing guidance for variable selection for the UARM algorithm. For example, (a) target approach speed deviation, (b) flap position, (c) landing gear position, (d) engine speed, (e) altitude above ground level (AGL), and (f) glide path deviation were variables stated in the FAA stable approach criteria categories. Adherence to stable approach criteria was determined based on the data, including: (a) the vertical and lateral position of the aircraft with reference to the landing runway, (b) energy state, and (c) landing configuration. The information gathered in the data analysis was then used to develop models to predict the probability of the pilot misperceiving the runway excursion risk of continuing an unstable approach to landing. Pilot risk misperception was suggested by the decision to continue to a landing even when evidence exists of exceedance in any one or more of the flight data variables from the stabilized approach criteria.

An advantage regarding internal validity of the study was the restriction to FDR data from one air carrier, one type of aircraft, and one FAA certified FDR. This limitation favorably decreased the likelihood of selection bias regarding feature selection and the application of FAA stable approach criteria. For example, the three constructs (energy state, landing configuration, and aircraft location relative the landing runway) were based on exceedance criteria to flight data variables from only one aircraft type. These findings were not unexpected as the literature indicated that deviations in energy management were frequently found to be contributing factors in runway excursions (FAA, 2014).

Variable importance was determined using the best performing model, DT. Findings indicate that six important variables stood out in the prediction of UARM. Glideslope Deviation (GLS) was the most important variable in the prediction model. The other important predictor variables in order of worth: (2) selected airspeed, (3) localizer deviation, (4) flaps not extended, (5) drift angle, and (6) approach speed deviation. Interpretation and effects of these important predictors to the probability of the occurrence of UARM are as follows:

- ***Glideslope deviation.*** Exceedance of glideslope deviation limits was also interpreted to be evidence of energy mismanagement. High deviations would support the exceedance of other high ranked variables regarding excessive energy and was also interpreted to support indications by other exceedance variable importance rankings that indicated energy mismanagement. This variable supports the high approach path that demonstrated high and fast at the assessment point.

- *Approach speed deviation.* The inclusion of airspeed deviations also supported the interpretation of energy mismanagement. The exceedance of approach speed limitations provided additional evidence of high and fast energy mismanagement. When combined with other important predictors of UARM, this flight variable provided support when combined with other important predictors regarding hazard of runway excursion.
- *Selected Calibrated Approach Speed.* A new finding that indicated the pilot selection of approach speed was an important predictor in UARM. The literature did not provide information of pilot selection of airspeed as an important predictor involved in either unstable approaches or runway excursions. The inclusion of this flight data variable represented a new discovery in the analysis of unstable approaches and pilot risk misperception of runway excursions. Significance of pilot selected approach in the prediction of UARM was a key indicator in approach speed deviation contributory factors to unstable approaches and the suggested lapse in ADM. Deviations between approach speed actually flown and selected approach speed were determined to be important in the prediction of UARM.
- *Localizer deviation and drift angle.* These two variables indicated exceedance in lateral relative position with the landing runway. Although not a direct indicator of energy mismanagement, lateral exceedances were interpreted to indicate risk misperception of runway excursion (veer off) that could have resulted from inaccurate runway alignment for landing.
- *Flaps.* This variable was of key importance supporting the energy mismanagement at the assessment point. If a pilot has the landing flaps at a 0 setting (flaps not deployed) at 500 feet, difficulty in maintaining approach

speed and rate of descent would be expected. This variable exceedance supported the interpretation that a combination of flaps up and speed brakes deployed indicated a risk misperception in ability to reduce energy prior to landing.

Exceedances in GS, runway alignment (LOC and DA) and excessive airspeed were noted as off nominal (i.e., FAA exceedance criteria) energy management. As such, analysis of those variables indicating a flight path trajectory of *high and fast* supported the assertion by the NTSB that energy mismanagement issues were contributory factors in many accidents/incidents involving runway excursions (NTSB, 2008; 2016). Findings supported those of NTSB in several accidents and incidents described in previous sections. Pilots attempting to reduce energy with incorrect lift device deployment (speed brakes) was determined to be a contributory factor in American Airlines 1420 as well as several other incidents including runway excursions (NTSB, 2001).

The findings fill the gaps in the literature for: (a) federal guidelines and oversight of hazards associated with unstable approaches and runway excursions, (b) aviation research conducted on pilot risk perception and risk tolerance, and (c) aviation research using predictive modelling based on advanced ML techniques applied to large FDR data. While the literature review described many examples of aviation research in each of these topics, the research filled the gaps as follows:

Unstable approach and runway excursion hazards. Findings of the study supported those provided by the FAA, NTSB, and FSF. These entities described in detail oversight, guidance, and/or recommendations to operators regarding the hazards associated with mitigating the risk of runway excursions. The FAA had listed unstable approaches as one of the most common causal factors in runway excursions (FAA, 2014). The FSF and NTSB corroborated this assertion that stable approaches (and safe landings) begin early in the approach planning phase of flight (FSF, 2009; NTSB, 2016, 2019b). Findings in the study concurred with these organizations that exceedances in stable approach criteria had been demonstrated with the analysis of large volumes of recorded flight data. Interpretation of the results of important flight variable predictors of UARM supported the recommendations by the NTSB for the necessity of more focused data-driven training in pilot ADM regarding risk perception.

Results of the study supported the FAA and NSTB call for improved pilot training initiatives, enhanced CRM training, as well as research into risk mitigation strategies for operators to avoid the hazards associated with unstable approaches (FAA, 2017a; NTSB, 2016, 2019b). Although the recorded flight data used in the research was insufficient to determine any actual occurrences of REs, results of important predictors indicated consistent energy mismanagement (high and fast) which were listed as contributory factors in runway excursions (runway overruns) in several incidents/accidents by the NTSB. This interpretation also supported the discovery in recent aviation accidents that had demonstrated unstable approaches continue to be causal factors. Results of the study also supported the NTSB recommendation that the aviation industry should respond to the hazard of unstable approaches with improvements in pilot training, as well as the development of CRM techniques to enhance pilot risk assessment and perception in flight operations (NTSB, 2013, 2019b).

Pilot risk perception and risk tolerance. Findings of the study successfully addressed the recommendation for future research by You and Han (2013), who recommended that potential factors affecting pilot lapses in ADM should be investigated. The researchers had also concluded that the safe operational behavior of pilots could be affected by HF characteristics such as ADM, HIP, SA, interpersonal communications and teamwork attitudes. Identification of potential indications of lapses in pilot ADM, particularly those involving risk misperception associated with energy mismanagement on approach were demonstrated. Results corroborated those of Hunter (2005) regarding the correlation between pilot risk perception and hazardous events. Actions by pilots regarding energy management risk misperception were interpreted to have indicated the potential overestimation of ability to reduce energy for landing. Excessive airspeed, rate of descent, and high on glidepath with a continuance to landing, rather than a rejected landing, suggested risk misperception. Results supported the conclusions of Hunter (2009), who asserted that pilot attitudes associated with perception of risk were strongly related to the relative levels of safety inherent in airline operations. Findings also addressed recommendations from Hunter (2009) and addressed gaps in the literature regarding the need for future research in pilot risk perception. Hunter (2009) specifically called for future research to be conducted to identify key factors that contribute to inaccurate perceptions of risk, which was one of the successful accomplishments of the research.

Predictive modeling using recorded flight data. Results of the study addressed gaps in the literature that were identified regarding anomaly detection in large flight data. Findings were in agreement with those of Bharadwaj et al. (2013), who detailed a multifaceted process of discovering and describing unusual events as Anomaly Detection. An area of agreement with Bharadwaj et al. (2013) indicated that anomaly detection was achievable in large flight data with the successful investigation to detect unusual events. One area of difference was that results did not support the use of cluster analysis to identify anomalies, but rather used standardized exceedance criteria. For example, an unstable approach was considered an anomaly in the context of this research, as defined by any exceedance of limitations presented in FAA AC 120-71A. However, results of the research did support the notion that anomaly detection could be described using events that did not fall into normal regions of expectations or standards.

One key difference with results provided by Li et al. (2015) and Aslaner, Unal, and Iyigun (2016) was that the current study demonstrated how SMEs should not necessarily be needed for interpretation and classification tasks. The successful demonstration of the use of standardized FAA exceedance criteria and the scalability of the UARM algorithm precluded the need for SME interpretation of exceedance criteria used in anomaly detection. Other differences in substance with the works of Li et al. (2015) and Aslaner, Unal, and Iyigun (2016) were noted. These researchers applied clustering techniques, rather than standardized exceedance criteria, to flight data to identify anomalies in the takeoff and landing phases of flight.

Findings addressed the gap demonstrated in these works that included a vague description of what constitutes abnormal flight events, variables of interest in the clustering analysis, and the lack of a clearly defined target variable. Findings also addressed deficiencies concerning the lack of a clearly described coding process. Another result was the successful demonstration of the use of a repeatable coding process, that was then used to build the models used in the evaluation of the algorithms. Conversely, results corroborated findings in the literature with the successful investigation into the application of advanced ML techniques to large FDR data to discover previously unknown anomalies, as recommended by Li et al. (2015) and Aslaner, Unal, and Iyigun (2016),

Results supported those of Gera and Goel (2015), who suggested that data mining was part of a more general process based on the discovery of knowledge pertaining to large data. Results also successfully addressed recommendations by Tong et al. (2018), who suggested that future research should use large FDM data to explore and discover anomalous events in the NAS. One area of disagreement was the assertion by Tong et al. (2018) that random forest, rather than decision tree models, were best suited to extract the most important features in predicting a target variable, landing speed in their case.

The demonstration of the capability of knowledge discovery process research model to discover important predictors of flight trajectory prediction was an important result. Additional results concurred with and supported the conclusions of Gallego et al. (2018), who produced research with the objective of investigating the effects of operational input variables on the vertical flight path trajectory prediction. Conclusions also supported findings with Kang and Hansen (2018) and Achenbach and Spinler (2018) that future research should incorporate weather-related data for improving accuracy of the predictive models.

Findings of the study built on those provided by Oehling and Barry (2019), who presented the use of ML techniques to detect unknown occurrences in flight data, generated by approximately 300 aircraft, from six different Airbus A320 fleets and sub-fleets, for over 1000 flights per day, from March 2013 to March 2016. Results support assertions by the researchers that methods enhancing the safety knowledge discovery process could be applied to large flight data. The research also built of the results obtained by Oehling and Barry (2019), who described ML in terms of algorithms which learn from the data.

Results of analysis described the strong predictive probability of UARM by the DT model as 98%. A sensitivity and specificity analysis was conducted that indicated a true positive prediction of 95% and a true negative prediction of 99%. These findings supported those of Maxson (2018), Truong et al. (2018), Oehling and Barry (2019), who asserted that models with predictive power above 90% indicated a high level of predictive performance. Considering the high predictive power of the best model, findings indicate that the AVSKD research model was acceptable to address the objectives of the study.

Findings demonstrating the ability to predict hazards supported that FAA assertion that effective SRM strategies should incorporate predictive risk identification and mitigation. For example, the ability to predict the probability of future occurrences of UARM could be useful in the successful safety risk mitigation strategies regarding the risk of runway excursions. Traditional SMS strategies have focused on *reactive* and *proactive* mitigation strategies. FAA guidelines suggested the development of predictive techniques in the SRM component of an organization's SMS. The FAA recommended that operators should be able to identify safety issues and spot trends before they result in an incident or accident. The evolution of SMS strategies has resulted in the requirement for carriers to develop and implement *predictive* risk management (FAA, 2007a). A SMS strategy favoring predictive methods rather than reactive methods is depicted in Figure 4.

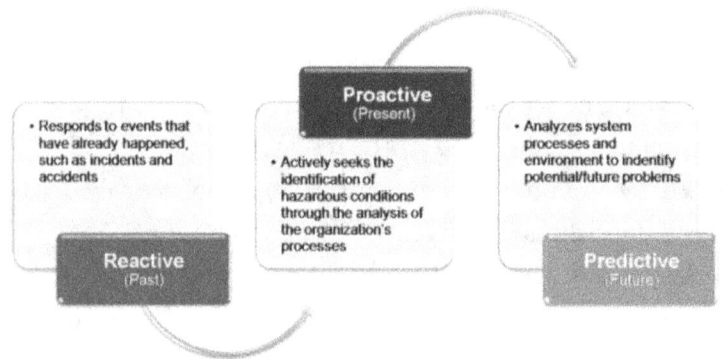

Figure 4. FAA predictive Safety Risk Mitigation strategy. Reprinted from "Safety Management System," by Federal Aviation Administration, 2016. Retrieved from https://www.faa.gov/about/initiatives/sms/explained/basis/

Conclusions

Continuation of an unstable approach to a landing had been identified by civil aviation authorities and the airline industry as one of the primary contributory factors to runway excursion hazards (FAA, 2014; NTSB, 2019b). Although the FAA had stipulated that operators adhere to criteria defining stable approaches, results corroborated industry data that unstable approaches still occur with some pilots not often following the FAA guidance to perform a rejected landing (FSF, 2009). Results indicated that 6% of unstable approaches resulted in a rejected landing, also supported this assertion. Additionally, agreement was noted with FAA-provided LOSA data, which indicated that 97% of unstable approaches resulted in a safe landing and that 3% of unstable approaches resulted in rejected landings (FAA, 2013). With the advent and deployment of advanced digital data recording devices, required under 14CFR §91.609 for all air carriers with an operating certificate, opportunities existed to analyze recorded flight data. Concurrently, recent developments in complex mathematical machine learning algorithms have improved research capability regarding the analysis of these flight data. The successful development and deployment of the UARM algorithm used in the research demonstrated the power and precision that such capabilities could achieve. Data mining techniques, both exploratory and predictive, can provide aviation researchers with the tools necessary to both analyze these large flight data and also to predict abnormal flight occurrences.

Results also successfully demonstrated how the UARM algorithm could be used to identify models that accurately and precisely predicted the probability of pilot misperception of runway excursion risk based on stabilized approach criteria, as well as the identification of important flight variables associated with frequent non-compliance of rejected landing guidelines. The UARM algorithm was also successfully used to identify important predictors of the occurrence of pilot risk misperception of runway excursion risk.

Theoretical contributions. Gaps in the literature were addressed through the demonstration of a reliable and valid methodology to predict pilot *Unstable Approach Risk Misperception*. Although hazards have been identified with the continued occurrences of runway excursions, the literature indicated that a reliable and valid representation of rejected landing decision-making based on unstable approach criteria had not been fully investigated. Results addressed this gap with the investigation of potential pilot lapses in aeronautical decision-making, specifically in the rejected landing following an unstable approach. Previous studies that have applied advanced data mining techniques to investigate and analyze large flight data have focused primarily on the validation and evaluation of advanced mathematical algorithms. Another important accomplishment was the demonstration of a predictive capability that could be used to mitigate the risk of *Unstable Approach Risk Misperception*.

Two factors indicating opportunities for research became evident with a review of the literature. The first factor was the large amount of data that are being recorded by advanced digital flight recorders on every commercial airline flight in the NAS. Airlines are encouraged by the FAA to voluntarily participate in the FOQA program. FOQA was designed to improve safety in commercial aviation by allowing airlines and pilots to share de-identified aggregate information with the FAA who can then monitor national trends in aircraft operations and focus its resources to address risk issues (e.g., flight operations, air traffic control (ATC), airports). Although voluntary (in the United States), the FOQA program has resulted in very large amounts of flight data that have not been accessed on a scale appropriate for these data. Even though pilot safety reports, accident reports, and safety debrief narratives constitute a large amount of data, the literature indicated that these data have only been explored with the use of text mining and qualitative methods. The research successfully addressed this gap with the demonstration of FDR data analysis and predictive model building. Previous studies relied on cluster analysis or exceedance criteria to discover abnormal flight events, but none offered a reliable and valid predictive model to predict *Unstable Approach Risk Misperception*.

The second factor that indicated opportunities for research was that although various statistical analytical methods have revealed clear patterns in the prediction of pilot performance, the literature indicated these data have not been exploited in order to fully investigate significant relationships of the predictors. An examination of the extant literature indicated a gap in research providing evidence of a relationship between pilot performance and flight anomaly variables. Previous studies described in the literature relied on results provided by the evaluation of subject matter experts, who were required to analyze the results and apply them to aviation problems. The research demonstrated the ability to predict *Unstable Approach Risk Misperception* without the necessity of subject matter expert analysis.

Algorithm development for predictive modeling. A key finding was the demonstration of the successful development and deployment of the UARM algorithm used in the predictive modeling process. The successful application of the AVSKD knowledge discovery process model to large recorded flight data using the UARM algorithm was also a significant finding. The scalability of the UARM algorithm allowed for use of multiple sets of flight data variables to determine pilot risk misperception of runway excursion risk. Additional findings were the discovery of the important predictors of UARM.

Results of the knowledge discovery process suggested that pilot risk misperception, specifically regarding energy mismanagement, had a strong relationship with the target variable, UARM. New predictors were flight variables specifically associated with energy management exceedances. Although airbrakes deployed and excessive approach speed were previously reviewed in the literature, key findings of the research included the discovery of additional new important predictors of UARM based on energy mismanagement of being high and fast (flaps up and excessive approach speed deviations). The discoveries of new important predictors of pilot risk misperception of runway excursion risk was a key result of the research.

These results provided the successful demonstration that flight data variables could be used to develop the algorithm for UARM. Once this determination was realized, a coding process was developed to create a data variable representing landing, rejected landing, and UARM. An important development in the study was that of a straightforward If/Then decision process used to construct the UARM algorithm (See Figure 8)

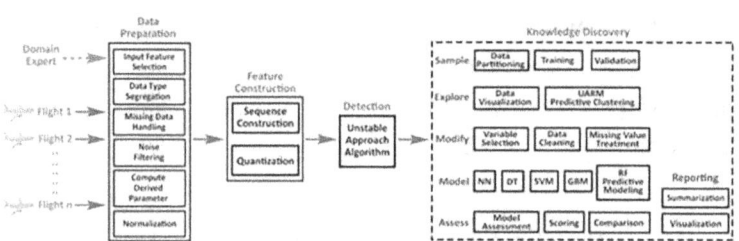

Figure 8. Research procedure framework. UARM = Unstable Approach Risk Misperception; NN = neural network; DT = decision tree; SVM = support vector machine; GBM = gradient boost machine; RF = random forest. Adapted from "Discovering Anomalous Aviation Safety Events Using Scalable Data Mining Algorithms," by B. Matthews, S. Das, K. Bhaduri, K. Das, R. Martin, and N. Oza, 2013, Journal of Aerospace Information Systems, 10(10), p. 469. Copyright 2013 by the Journal of Aerospace Information System, and from "Prediction of Airport Arrival Rates Using Data Mining Methods" (Doctoral Dissertation) by R. W. Maxson, 2018, p. 70. Copyright 2018 by R. W. Maxson.

Results of this If/Then assessment process were successful in the identification that evidence of UARM had occurred or not.

For example, once an unstable approach was identified, a determination was made whether or not a rejected landing was performed. If evidence of an unstable approach was indicated, and a rejected landing was not performed, then UARM resulted. Results of this UARM algorithm development were then successfully used to construct predictive models as well as the identification of UARM. The rest of the flight data variables, including those representing the FAA stable approach criteria, were utilized as input variables and were anticipated to be continuous or categorical. For example, approach speed was expected be continuous, based on numerical values while landing gear position was expected to be categorical (i.e. either up or down).

Results indicated that one advantage of the UARM algorithm was that of scalability. Several different predictive models successfully utilized the UARM algorithm with the application of recorded flight data. Results demonstrated that real world recorded flight data was successfully assessed in the UARM algorithm process to predict the probability of occurrence of the target variable. The UARM algorithm was successfully and repeatedly used with consistent results to evaluate large recorded flight data. The algorithm was successfully developed based on initial data coding, subsequent use of an If/Then decision-making process, and ultimately the extremely accurate and precise predictive power regarding the target variable, UARM. The UARM algorithm provided a step-by-step, repeatable process to the analysis of recorded flight data and allowed for a reliable and valid methodology for the analysis of FDR data to predict UARM.

Practical contributions. Key beneficiaries of the research are airline pilot simulator training programs and airline Safety Management System managers. The ability of airline pilot training managers to not only predict UARM but also identify hazardous trends in aircraft state variables involved in ADM could have a positive impact on airline safety risk mitigation strategies inherent in pilot simulator training programs, such as the development of realistic runway excursion scenarios. Results of the study could be used to further refine not only FAA (2014) stabilized approach criteria but also in the FAA oversight of air carrier pilot training programs.

Safety Management Systems managers could use the results to improve SRM effectiveness, as required under 14CFR Part 5. Because SMS programs have traditionally relied on hazard identification using accident and incident reports rather than predictive measures, predictive capabilities could be beneficial (FAA, 2007a). The ability to predict UARM could provide SMS managers with a predictive tool that would enhance safety risk mitigation effectiveness.

Unstable approaches and runway excursion hazards. Results support positions taken by the FAA, NTSB, and FSF, who have provided oversight, guidance, and/or recommendations to operators regarding the hazards associated with mitigating the risk of runway excursions. Results indicated that unstable approaches, followed by failure of the pilot to execute a rejected landing, continued to occur in the NAS. Interpretation of these results leads one to conclude that efforts to improve training and awareness of the runway excursion hazard have been ineffective. Recommendations for improved pilot training initiatives, enhanced CRM training, as well as research into risk mitigation strategies for operators to avoid the hazards associated with unstable approaches have seemingly not addressed the critical factors (FAA, 2017a; NTSB, 2016, 2019b). Results support evidence of pilot energy mismanagement, which had been discovered to be among contributory factors in runway excursions in recent aviation accidents and incidents (Campbell et al., 2018). Results concur with and support the position taken by the NTSB, which had recommended that the aviation industry respond to the hazard of unstable approaches with improvements in pilot training, as well as the development of CRM techniques to enhance pilot risk assessment and perception in flight operations (NTSB, 2013; 2019b).

Limitations of the findings

The findings should be interpreted for external validity in the context of the following: (a) normal cockpit procedures; (b) calm weather; (c) uncontaminated runway with proper approach and runway lighting; (d) no pilot physiological anomalies; (e) no failures or degradation of aircraft equipment/systems; (f) fully operational navigational aids, (g) crews exercising proper CRM, and (h) proper use of automation, as supported by the 2013 FAA report *Operational Use of Flight Deck Automation Systems* (FAA, 2013). These limitations provided stimulation for recommendations for future research as well as recommendations to the target population.

Recommendations

The ability of airline pilot training managers to not only predict UARM but also identify hazardous trends in aircraft state variables involved in ADM could have a positive impact on airline safety risk mitigation strategies inherent in pilot simulator training programs, such as developing realistic scenarios for an unstable approach resulting in a runway excursion. Additionally, Safety Management Systems managers should use the predictive capabilities to support the FAA mandate for SRM to be proactive in identifying and mitigating hazards. SMS programs have traditionally relied on hazard identification using accident and incident reports rather than predictive measures.

Recommendations for the target population. Results suggested that advances in airline pilot simulator training programs were necessary. Findings indicate that unstable approaches were followed by a landing occurred at a rate of 94%. Regulatory guidance has been provided and the hazard identified, yet the risk misperception of unstable approaches has not been successfully mitigated. The ability of airline pilot training managers to not only predict UARM but also identify hazardous trends in aircraft state variables involved in ADM could have a positive impact on airline safety risk mitigation strategies inherent in pilot simulator training programs, such as developing realistic runway excursion scenarios.

Recommendation 1. Airline pilot training managers should develop simulator training scenarios to address potential pilot lapses in aeronautical decision making regarding Unstable Approach Risk Misperception based on an analysis of recorded flight data. For example, results suggested that pilots facing evidence of unstable approach regarding energy mismanagement attempted to reduce energy with deployement of speed brakes and idle power settings, rather than reject the landing. Improved simulator training could assist pilots in the recognition of energy mismanagement, and the associated hazard of runway excurion based on being *high and fast* (Campbell et al., 2018; FAA, 2013) A goal of this enhanced training should be the goal of improving ADM resulting in increased likelihood of rejected landing when faced with evidence of unstable approach.

Recommendation 2. Airline industry Safety Management System managers should develop strategies, based on an analysis of recorded flight data, to better mitigate unstable approaches by identifying conditions where pilots misperceive the risk. SMS managers should use safety awareness initiatives regarding pilot risk misperception of runway excursion risk. Organizational safety culture should be enhanced to alleviate potential lapses in ADM regarding *Unstable Approach Risk Misperception. Pilots* should be made more aware of the notion that a rejected landing is a successful outcome regarding unstable approach, which should also be supported by air carrier management.

Recommendations for future research. Future research involving data mining, machine learning algorithms, and predictive modeling should focus on more comprehensive flight data sets, not only aircraft state variables, to better represent the complex operational environment. Based on the unexpected result of the identification of selected Mach early in the iterative variable importance investigation, factors related to other phases of flight could be important predictors of UARM. This result was unexpected as selected Mach was not observed to have contributed to the literature on unstable approaches or runway excursion contributory factors. Mach speed is a flight variable associated with the cruise phase of flight, rather than approach and landing variables. Therefore, it is recommended that all phases of flight should be investigated, not only the approach and landing phase, to determine if other factors and co-variates contribute to UARM. For example, analysis of pilot descent planning and instrument approach briefings could reveal additional factors contributing to *Unstable Approach Risk Misperception*. Safety risk mitigation strategies should be included in the predictive model. Furthermore, existing pilot alerting technologies such as Terrain Awareness and Warning System (TAWS) and other technologies that alert the pilot of incorrect aircraft configuration or excessive rate of descent, should be incorporated into the model in order to investigate potential risk reduction strategies.

Recommendation 3. Develop more thorough and comprehensive models that extend beyond recorded flight data sets, to other data sets such as cockpit voice recorder data (e.g. crew/ATC coordination information) affecting decision-making, and weather data for external conditions (e.g. turbulence, wind-shear) affecting aircraft state variables. Predictive modeling of flight events should be enhanced with more thorough replication of those factors which could influence pilot ADM. For example, weather conditions, including runway condition (ice or wet) should be included in flight data in order to enhance and improve predictive capability of models.

Results of the study supported the literature provided by FAA, NTSB, FSF, and IATA in terms of low SOP compliance rates regarding the unstable approach rejected landing decision-making process. Future research should include the investigation of the effects of not only CRM issues, but automation interface. Findings provided by Giles (2013) were supported by the results of this study with the suggestion that low SOP compliance rates could indicate pilot to machine interface issues. Giles also suggested that safety culture should be investigated for effects on low SOP compliance rates regarding the rejected landing ADM process.

Recommendations for future testing support those of Achenbach and Spinler (2018), who stated that significant limitations to their study were the lack of real-time weather data, the omission of crew resource management considerations as well as ATC flow control in the construction of predictive models. For example, weather data (e.g. turbulence/convective activity) and ADM aspects of CRM could enhance the knowledge discovery process in the prediction of UARM and should be included in studies predicting pilot risk misperception.

Recommendation 4. Develop and enhance predictive pilot alerting technologies regarding unstable approaches to mitigate runway excursions. Pilot alerting technologies have been previously developed to mitigate various risks, such as controlled flight into terrain, landing with gear up, and landing with evidence of windshear. Similar technological developments should be pursued that would alert pilots when unstable approach conditions are evident and a rejected landing should be executed. For example, AI should be further developed and utilized to enhance current certified technology such as Honeywell's SmartLanding™ and other systems currently under development. AI technology improvements to current systems should be further developed to comply with FAA recommendations shifting current SRM strategies from reactive and proactive to predictive (FAA, 2016).

AVIATION RESEARCH USING MINING TECHNIQUES

Data mining methods

With the rapid accumulation of large data becoming more available to researchers, opportunities for the exploration of these data have manifested themselves. FOQA and FDR data provide an appropriate source for the application of data mining methods. Much of the early work of examining these large flight data was accomplished with the intent of validating, comparing, and identifying the most accurate models of the system being evaluated. As the body of knowledge grew, so did the techniques and applications of data mining.

Early examples of research applying data mining methods to flight data show that much of the work was done on validating complex algorithms, with limited results on the identification of patterns or significant relationships hidden in the large data. The work of Mugtussidis (2000) provides one such example of the limitations inherent in early efforts to analyze flight data. Mugtussidis describes the challenges associated with feature selection and proposed a classification process using estimated probability density functions.

Limitations in the research represent obstacles typical of flight data analysis techniques before the advent and deployment of advanced ML algorithms. The author recommends that as computational capabilities improve, that more optimal search techniques be utilized. Mugtussidis continues to recommend that flights are segmented using cluster analysis allowing unusual events to be more accurately discovered. As the research progressed, more work began to evolve into the use of data mining to provide results which could be applied to the identification of hazards.

Finally, with the development of data mining techniques, the feasibility of building complex predictive models evolved. Li, Das, Hansman, Palacios, and Srivastava (2015) present research concerning cluster-based anomaly detection to identify abnormal flight events. The results were then examined by subject matter experts, who then classified the events regarding level of hazard. Their research was enabled using large data gathered from over 26,000 commercial airline flights. Clustering techniques were then applied to the data to identify anomalies in the takeoff and landing phases of flight. The research was designed using two experimental methods: one to sample 91 flight parameters in the effort to identify abnormal flight events, and a second to evaluate three different data clustering algorithms. Limitations to the study include a vague description of what constitutes abnormal flight events, as well as those variables of interest in the clustering analysis, and the lack of a clearly defined target variable. It is also unclear what coding was used to build the models used in the evaluation of the algorithms. Additionally, the SMEs used in the evaluation of the abnormal flight events do not apply any standard criteria in their analysis.

Wang, Wu, and Sun (2014) provide a landmark study on the use of Tianjin Airlines B737 QAR based flight data research on RE impact factors. The researchers determine that pilot flare technique and weather factors are significantly correlated to RE hazards. Although the research is based on a limited sample size, the findings indicate that reactive modeling can provide important results regarding feature selection. Nanduri and Sherry (2016) build on the research of Wang et al. but limit their study to the use simulated FOQA-like flight data to investigate landing excursion hazards into San Francisco International Airport. The researchers use X-Plane simulated flight data to construct recurrent NN models using 21 flight variables. The researchers were able to demonstrate the performance of NN models in anomaly detection of FOQA-like data but used a very small sample size and applied vague exceedance criteria. They recommend that future research increase the number of flight variables and build models with different feature combinations.

Aslaner, Unal, and Iyigun (2016) present research based on the application of data mining methods to FDR data in order to identify safety issues in commercial flight operations. Specifically, cluster analysis techniques were applied to a sample of landing phase of flight operations airline data, although the source of the sample and population were not identified. Dynamic time warping (DTW) was introduced as a cluster analysis technique based on unsupervised learning and was used to examine FDM data and unstable approaches were filtered. A key factor of this research is that DTW was shown to adequately classify landings at different airports and runways and that different events could be grouped with respect to the similarities. Another meaningful aspect of the study is that the DTW method, which was used to approximate the distances between the landing performance variables, was not adversely affected by small variations in the same type of data. Limitations of the study are the relatively small sample size, poorly defined population, and lack of generalizability. Also, the data source was not specifically identified, and the phase of flight was poorly defined by reliable criteria.

Friso, Richard, Visser, Vincent, and Bruno (2018) build on Li's research with their paper on the use of ML methods to predict abnormal runway occupancy times, based on radar data patterns.

Sampling and data sources were gathered using final approach radar data and A-SMGCS runway data consisting of 78,321 flights at Paris Charles de Gaulle airport and were compared with 500,000 flights at Vienna airport. Machine learning was used in feature selection and regression was used to observe the important precursors, which were identified from the top 10 features. The study focused on two different time window predictions. The first one made predictions based on abnormal arrival runway occupancy time (AROT) and associated precursors. The second one made predictions on arrival sequences for terminal air traffic flow based on a one to two-hour window. The researchers argue that the usefulness of these predictions could lead to an improvement in runway safety and throughput. The significance of the results of the research was the demonstration of the use of combined ML techniques to forecast arrival runway occupancy time (AROT) per flight. A limitation of the study was the restriction of the scope to arrival runway occupancy data.

Shi, Guan, Zurada, and Manikas (2017) detail how data mining (DM) methods can be utilized in aviation safety management system programs. Specifically, data-mining methods were applied to identify risk factors in commercial aviation by sampling pilot narratives from the NASA ASRS. The researchers initially used topical mining methods to convert the pilot narratives to model input. ML algorithms were then used to incrementally build and assess classification models for risk factor identification. Three different classification algorithms were evaluated. Results indicated the effectiveness for inclusion in an organization's SMS. A limitation of the study was the focus was primarily on the justification of the evaluation methods for various algorithms, rather than on the identification of aviation safety hazard applications.

Finally, *Maxson (2018)* and *Truong, Friend, and Chen (2018)* apply data mining methods in their research on flight delay prediction. These studies are particularly significant regarding the building, evaluation, and comparison of various models with the intent of the prediction of flight delays. Specifically, Truong et al. (2018) used FAA Aviation System Performance Matrix (ASPM) data, which were sampled in order to apply decision tree and Bayesian inference modelling, in order to predict the probability of a flight-delay incidents. Maxson (2018) focused his analysis on arrival delays based on input variables related to weather phenomena. Although the sampling of Truong et al. was limited to on-time data at Newark and Miami International Airport and Maxson considered only 10 airports in the NAS, the demonstration of data mining methods in the prediction of a target variable was found to be significant.

Text mining methods

Matthews et al. (2013) developed research on both topic and data mining. The researchers applied these methods to both pilot narrative safety reports as well as flight data. Significant aspects of the study include the description of the Aviation Safety Knowledge Discovery Process (AVSKD). The context of their study demonstrates the use of a structured knowledge discovery process, which harmonizes DM methods in order to identify precursors to aviation safety incidents. Their research used data samples based on raw FOQA data, from aircraft operating in the NAS collected from takeoff to landing. The typical flight generated 5000-6000 samples and 350 flight parameters. DM methods include scalable multiple-kernel learning algorithm for anomaly detection. Significant findings of the research include the application and validation of data mining methods to large commercial aviation datasets to detect precursors to aviation safety events. A limitation of the study was the restriction to data from one aircraft fleet type, thus limiting the generalizability of the results.

Christopher, Vivekanandam, Anderson, Markkandeyan, and Sivakumar (2016); Koteeswaran, Malarvizhi, Kannan, Sasikala, and Geetha (2017); and *Kuhn (2018)* present the application of text mining techniques to accident data reports.

Arockia et al. (2016) developed a classification model for aviation risk mitigation techniques using decision tree methods. While Koteeswaran et al. (2017) also applied several data mining methods to accident report narratives, distinct aspects of the research include the investigation of correlation-based feature selection (CFS) using an oscillating search technique (OST). This technique was used to select attributes that could be important factors in contributory accident causal identification. Both studies utilized feature selection, which is normally done by searching attribute subsets and evaluating each one, and decision tree and Bayesian networks for classification of aircraft accident factors. The studies contrast in the findings of model accuracy effectiveness.

Christopher et al. (2016) concluded that decision tree models performed the best regarding classification accuracy and lower error rates in misclassification, while Koteeswaran et al. (2017) determined that cluster computing, using the feature selection algorithm, Improved Oscillating Correlation based Feature Selection (IOCFS), was superior to decision tree models, in terms of classification accuracy. Limitations to these studies are the reactive nature of hazard identification and the lack of predictive capabilities inherent in their modelling techniques.

Finally, *Kuhn (2018)* builds on previous research with the use of structural topic modeling NASA ASRS data. A key feature of the research is that although the study continues with previous work on the classification of accident causal factors, results also revealed the ability to identify and predict relationships in aircraft accident contributory factors. Even though the study was limited to ASRS narratives involving fuel system and landing gear anomalies, results also revealed unstable approaches to San Francisco International Airport. The unintended identification of unstable approach instances provides an opportune juncture in the body of knowledge for the investigation of flight data monitoring (FDM) or FOQA data for the purpose of addressing unstable approach occurrence and how to predict these occurrences.

Machine learning predictive models

Data Mining

While data mining is a relatively broad term, a key descriptor includes computer-driven data analysis techniques and applies artificial intelligence in the exploration of large data in order to discover patterns or relationships that might be used in predictive modelling. Large, messy data sources may be "cleaned" and structured in a more feasible format for the purposes of applying data mining techniques. Models can then be constructed in order to represent theoretical relationships of interest. The models can subsequently be used as a comparison tool to try and justify evidence for further analysis (Dubey, Kamath, & Kanakia, 2016).

Gera and Goel (2015) assert that data mining is part of a more general process based on the discovery of knowledge pertaining to large data. They further describe the idea that several sources of data can be exploited simultaneously and introduce the concept of dynamic and static sources of data. Dynamic data sets, like those generated by FDR data of commercial aircraft operations in the NAS, are particularly important to aviation research. The use of dynamic data could be appropriate in applications with continuously changing environmental conditions inherent in the NAS.

Al Ghoson (2011) compares the strengths and weaknesses of several commercially available tools in the application of DM techniques: SAS® Enterprise MinerTM, SPSS® ClementineTM, and the IBM DB2® Intelligent MinerTM. The researchers assert that many business application packages favor decision tree and clustering analyses in the decision-making process. Their research criteria included the following in their evaluation: a) performance,

b) functionality, c) usability, and d) auxiliary task support. Based on these criteria, the researcher concludes that SAS® Enterprise MinerTM encompasses nearly all aspects of data mining, to include: text mining, simulation, predictive modeling, optimization, and experimental designs.

Bharadwaj et al. (2013) detail a multifaceted process of discovering and describing unusual events as Anomaly Detection. They use the term synonymously with unusual occurrences, outliers, and surprises. The researchers further assert that the process encompasses several attributes, including the type of anomaly, the nature of the data, and the handling of uncertainty inherent in the system. Contextual anomalies describe abnormal occurrences as defined by guidelines or expectations. For example, an unstable approach is considered an anomaly in the context of this research, as defined by any exceedance of limitations presented in FAA AC 120-71A and later AC 91-79A. Hence, anomaly detection can be described as occurrences that do not fall into normal regions of expectations or standards. In terms of complex systems with multiple regions of normal behaviors, such as flight operations (takeoff, cruise, descent, and approach and landing phases of flight), anomaly detection describes operations that do not fall into these regions. The researchers further assert that abnormal behaviors may appear as clusters that are discernible from normal clusters. Thus, these clusters can become the framework which describes clustering algorithms models.

Das, Mathews, and Lawrence (2011) and *Gorinevsky, Mathews and Martin (2012)* discuss machine learning methods as a basis for addressing data-driven anomaly detection problems associated with large data. Gorinevsky et al. (2012) describe the evolution of ML from traditional statistical process control (SPC) to supervised ML methods. Supervised ML methods utilize training data labeling in order to build predictive models to detect abnormalities. Examples of classification and regression supervised anomaly detection methods include: (a) decision tree, (b) neural network, (c) logistic regression, (d) SVM, (e) random forest, and (f) gradient boosting algorithms.

Decision tree

DTs are a flowchart type of decision support tool and have become popular in machine learning. It provides a visual representation in decision analysis also used in modeling event outcomes and is commonly used in ML processes to display algorithms consisting of conditional control statements (Tufféry, 2011). Decision tree models consist of internal nodes, which represent analysis on model attributes. Branches represent the results of the process, with each leaf node representing classification labels. Tufféry (2011) describes advantages of decision tree models as easy to understand and analyze, and can be conveniently combined with other analysis techniques. However, disadvantages include being relatively unstable and often inaccurate when compared with other techniques. Additionally, decision tree models tend to over fit and tend to bias favoring attributes with categorical variables.

Tufféry (2011) describes decision tree as an iterative process that divides a given population into segments, based on variables that encompass distinctive qualities within the population. The process begins with the formation of the root, or parent, node. Subsequent nodes are called child nodes, which are then further segregated into intermediate nodes, if applicable. The end cycle consists of terminal nodes, or leaves, which, when integrated with previous segments, indicate a branch of the tree. Training data are then used to calculate probabilities for each node. These probabilities are based on a node rule, which is established using the selection variable value set. These value sets are referred to as targets and a decision refers to the selection of a variable at each node. With business decision making applications, decision trees are typically used for the purposes of minimizing loss, maximizing profit, or to reduce classification error (Maxson, 2018; Sarma, 2013).

Maxson (2018) provides details on the use of decision tree predictive modeling in his study focusing on the prediction of arrival rates at 10 airports in the NAS.

Misclassification, lift, and ASE are used to determine tree value. Ultimately, the goal is to minimize cost and maximize profit regarding decisions. ASE is only appropriate in cases with a continuous target variable. Training, validation, and test datasets are partitioned based on the size of the sample. In cases of relatively small sample size, 40/30/30 or 50/25/25 percentage splits are used to train, validate, and test data subsets. The validation dataset is also commonly referred to as the pruning dataset. Larger training datasets usually result in consistent parameter estimates. The training dataset: assists selection based on specific guidelines at a node, conducts probability estimates at each node, and determines the decision variable value at the node. The tree is pruned using the validation dataset and the optimal tree generates the highest profit. Tree worth is determined by comparing splitting values. Performance assessment is based on the training data set and is used in model comparison (Maxson, 2018; Sarma, 2013).

Neural network

Often referred to as artificial neural networks (NN), they are models that process information between multiple layers. *Tufféry (2011)* describes the broad application of neural networks in the application of clustering, classification, and predictive model designs. The neural network model represents a series of source nodes that circuitously transport data to output layers of neurons. Additionally, intermediate layers may be found between the source nodes and output neurons that process data prior to the outer layers. Sarma (2013) asserts that a NN model transforms variables and performs model estimation. NN modeling is based on an iterative process, where the data source can be transformed and processed.

SAS Enterprise Miner has a menu of options which allow for the selection of a combination of hidden layer or target layer function, with each generating a new NN model (Sarma, 2013). The AutoNeural node can select activation functions for a variety of multilayer networks. The DM Neural node selects the highest performance rated input variables to fit a non-linear solution using R^2 assessment of the linear regression on the important input factors (Maxson, 2018).

Regression

With the examination of a binary target variable, logistic regression is recommended by Tufféry (2011) based on several factors. First, logistic regression can handle dependent variables with two values, without making as restrictive assumptions necessary. Logistic regression has been shown to be highly reliable, with the reliability relatively straightforward to monitor using several available statistical indicators. Logistic regression is also highly generalizable, widely interpretable, and robust. Tufféry (2011) describes several advantages of logistic regression: appropriate for discrete, qualitative, or continuous independent variables; ordinal or nominal dependent variables; requires less restrictive assumptions (compared with linear regression) of multinormality or homoscedasticity of the independent variables; and can provide very accurate models (Tufféry, 2011). Logistic regression also allows for interactions among independent variables. This is important to the research in that unstable approach criteria involve several independent variables. One of the most significant advantages of logistic regression is that it directly models a probability, which is a key point in the research. Although logistic regression has some disadvantages, such as the requirement that the explanatory variables must be linear independent, and sensitivity to missing values of continuous variables, these disadvantages are expected to have little impact to the research. Tufféry (2011) continues to suggest that regression analysis is very useful when the collinear relationships could exist among the important predictor variables or the observations are exceeded by the selection of variables.

Logistic regression analysis, or logit regression, consists of a logistic function to model a binary dependent target variable. The binary dependent target variable in the study, UARM, has only two possible outcomes, the presence of UARM, or the lack of presence of UARM, valued as "0" or "1". In the logistic regression model, the logarithm of the odds for the presence of UARM, or "1", is a linear combination of the independent, or predictor variables. The predictor variables can be either continuous or categorical.

The logistic function converts the log-odds to probability, with the unit of measurement being a logit, or logistical unit. Logistic regression was binomial in this research, meaning the target variable has only two possible outcomes, hence the target variable is a binary categorical variable. Binary logistic regression was used to predict the odds of UARM occurring based on the values of the independent predictor variables. Because logistic regression is used to predict a categorical target variable, rather than a continuous target variable, as in linear regression, the assumptions of linear regression may be discarded, particularly normal distribution of residuals, are violated (Tufféry, 2011).

Tufféry (2011) continues to assert that logistic regression is analogous to linear regression, but differs in the relationship between the independent and dependent variables. Significant differences include the prediction of values are probabilities, "0" or "1", rather than the values of the outcomes themselves. Subsequent descriptions of model fitting and regression coefficient estimating were provided in detail, as well as an examination of the contribution of individual predictors of UARM. The odds ratio was used to examine predictor effects on the exponential function of the regression coefficient (Tufféry, 2011). Several of the most notable tests of significance regarding important predictor variables are the likelihood ratio test and the Wald statistic (Tufféry, 2011).

Truong, Friend, and Chen (2018) support logistic regression methods with a contrasting description of multiple logistic regression. *Maxson (2018)* provides evidence supporting techniques used by the team, even though his research uses linear regression modeling with a continuous target variable. The researchers assert that multiple logistic regression is commonly used in predictive modeling and is an appropriate method to use to predict the value of a dependent variable based on multiple independent (predictor) variables. However, linear regression necessitates that no missing values be present, as well as the very restrictive assumptions on normality, linearity, homoscedasticity, and non-multicollinearity.

Although Tufféry (2011) continues to assert that while logistic regression is a form of multiple regression, an important distinction contrasting with the work of Maxson (2018) is that it has an outcome variable that is a categorical variable and predictor variables which are continuous or ordinal. Binary variables are present if only two categorical outcomes can result; with more than two possibilities, the regression is considered multi-nominal, or polychromous. The linearity assumptions are implicitly violated when a categorical dependent variable is chosen.

However, this issue can be overcome by transforming the data logarithmically. In other words, the binary dependent categorical variable is transformed into a continuous curve. While different approaches can be taken, generally it is assumed that the dependent variable is based on probabilistic outcomes that vary from zero to one. In a binary logistic regression, if the outcome probability is close to zero, the determination is that outcome "Y" did not occur, whereas if the outcome probability is close to one, the outcome "Y" did occur.

Sarma (2013) reports the SAS® Enterprise MinerTM software defaults to a logistic regression if the target variable is binary, ordinal, or nominal. If the target variable is binary, the regression defaults to logit link; if there are more than two categorical outcomes for an ordinal target variable a cumulative logits link is used, if there are more than two categorical outcomes for a nominal target variable a generalized logits link is employed. These include: (a) Akaike Information Criterion (AIC), (b) Schwarz Bayesian Criterion (SBC), (c) Validation Error, (d) Validation Misclassification, (e) Cross Validation Error, (f) Cross Validation Misclassification, (g) Validation Profit/Loss, (h) Profit/Loss, (i) Cross Validation Profit/Loss, or (j) no classification criterion.

Support vector machine (SVM)

This is a machine learning algorithm technique form of supervised learning. SVMs can be used in data analysis for classification and regression. An SVM model is built using a training algorithm involving an example training set of data. The data is partitioned into two categories, and the SVM algorithm can build a model that assigns data into one of the two categories. SVM models can be used as both non-probabilistic binary linear classifiers, as well as with probabilistic classifications. An SVM model provides a visual map of data points in space, depicted so that the data points representing the separate categories indicate a clear gap, as wide as possible. The data is then mapped into the model so that it can be predicted to fall into one of the two categories. SVMs can be used for both linear and non-linear classification. A kernel trick is used in non-linear classification SVMs, in order to depict the data into multi-dimensional feature (Chidambaram & Srinivasagan, 2018).

Oehling and Barry (2019) present the use of ML techniques to detect unknown occurrences in flight data, generated by approximately three hundred aircraft, from six different Airbus A320 fleets and sub-fleets, for over 1000 flights per day, from March 2013 to March 2016. The researchers introduce methods enhancing the safety knowledge discovery process. They continue to describe ML in terms of algorithms which learn from the data. The researchers assert that effective uses have been demonstrated with software which builds models, based on input data, rather than a predefined model which was encoded in the software during algorithm development. The study divides ML subcategories into both supervised and unsupervised learning. The contrasting categories are distinct in that supervised learning is based on previous knowledge of the solution. Unsupervised learning does not possess pre-knowledge but is commonly used to structure large data in clusters, or outliers. Other examples of unsupervised learning include: (a) outlier detection, (b) extreme value analysis, (c) probabilistic and statistical model-based approaches, (d) proximity-based approaches, (e) angle-based approaches, and (f) artificial neural network modeling. Specific goals of their ML methods addressed the following requirements:

- Detect unknown occurrences: The model should not rely on pre-determined criteria but use the entire data to find safety-related events. Contrasting exceedance monitoring systems, the goal is to detect previously unknown false negatives.
- Handle large data: The model should be able to process millions of flights and provide safety departments results within two to three days.
- Handle diverse data: The model should not be restricted to a limit on aircraft type or airports.
- Produce useful results: The model should have significant practical and theoretical implications. (Oehling and Barry, 2019, p. 90)

Lauer and Bloch (2008) assert that a key element in the incorporation SVMs as a state-of-the-art performance application regards two types of prior knowledge: class-variance and knowledge of the data. Class-variance applies to transformations, permutations and in domains of input space, contrasting with knowledge of unlabeled data, imbalances in the training set, or the quality of the data. The researchers continue to describe a recent method, which was developed for support vector regression, and considers prior knowledge on arbitrary regions of the input space. Significant contributions to the literature include the importance of prior knowledge in ML techniques implies that to gain improvements in model performance, some prior knowledge about the research problem is necessary. Specifically, Lauer and Bloch (2007) present three methods for incorporating prior knowledge:

- Sample methods: incorporate prior knowledge by either generating new data or modifying existing data accountability;
- Kernel methods: incorporate prior knowledge in the kernel function either by creating a new kernel or selecting the most appropriate one;
- Optimization methods: incorporate prior knowledge in the problem formation either with problem constraints or by defining a new formulation based intrinsically on the prior knowledge. (p. 1584)

Biswas, Mack, Mylaraswamy, and Bharadwaj (2013) describe machine learning approaches as a basis for addressing data-driven anomaly detection problems. The researchers assert that supervised and unsupervised machine learning methods can be effective to detect anomalies in nominal situations. Decision tree classifiers, neural network, regression, SVM, random forest, and gradient boosting are presented as examples of both types of anomaly detection methods. The researchers present a contrasting anomaly detection algorithm, which uses a semi-supervisory learning approach to explore fleet-wide aircraft flight data segments or phases in order to discover deviations from a nominal model of the data. The researchers continue to assert that human experts assist in the semi-supervised modeling process because of their effectiveness in preventing classifications errors based on differentiating criteria between nominal and abnormal.

Das et al. (2010, 2011) identify one-class SVM as a popular semi-supervised anomaly detection technique. The researchers describe the one-class SVM as an extension of SVM applications, which optimizes the classifier for a single class label. This optimization performs data segregation based on boundary criteria, based on the training data, and can suffer from limited information for the SME. Another difficulty described by the researchers concerns noisy training data creating a poor decision boundary in the classification process, thus introducing classification error in the modeling process. One mitigation strategy is for the SME to clearly define segregation criteria (Biswas et al., 2013).

A One-Class SVM classifier can be constructed from a Multiple Kernel Anomaly Detection (MKAD), semi-supervised method for anomaly detection. The algorithm processes the flight data into symbolic feature sequences, so that measures can be applied to comparing the similarity between samples. Das et al. (2010, 2011) describe this transformation as a significant challenge in the knowledge discovery process. The MKAD approach has been proven effective to the application of anomaly detection in FOQA data to a fleet of aircraft. The assumption that SVM is constructed from nominal data and used to discriminate and segregate non-nominal data. The researchers continue to show that SVM modeling has been effective in anomaly detection of flight data, with examples including high energy approaches, pilot responses to external environmental conditions, and high energy, low altitude flight conditions.

Mendes (2012) and *Smart (2012)* provide examples of supervised learning ML techniques using SVM to investigate 629 automatic landings and 1518 flights into one airport, respectively. Their research indicates that anomaly detection using ML techniques could be more efficient and effective when compared to conventional FDM methods of exceedance algorithm analysis. Ju and Tian (2012) discuss in more detail how the introduction of knowledge-based SVM via nearest point can incorporate prior knowledge in support vector machines. They assert that SVMs can be highly effective in the data mining process by constructing hyperplanes with a large separation margin, and hence, lower generalization error of the classification. The researchers demonstrate how effective measures can be used with prior knowledge by transforming boundary points in order to compute the shortest distances between the original training data and the knowledge data sets.

Hu, Zhou, Xie, and Chang (2016) establish a model to predict the occurrence of hard landing flight safety events. The researchers based their study of the use of QAR-collected flight data and determined that nine aircraft variables were relevant in landing phase. The featured variables used in the study were (a) radio altimeter height AGL, (b) aircraft pitch angle, (c) aircraft pitch angle rate of change, (d) groundspeed, (e) longitudinal distance to touchdown, (f) elevator flight control surface displacement, and (g) vertical acceleration. The team selected the *flight variable radio altimeter height AGL* to partition the flight data, and vertical speed was selected as the output variable. Thus, vertical acceleration was determined to be the target variable, or the predictive target, and the other variables were considered input data for the SVM model. Factor analysis was used to select relevant input variables to build the predictive model. An SVM predictive model was then constructed to predict the occurrence of hard landings.

Important results of the study include the confirmation that increased efficiency and accuracy of the predictive model, based on SVM techniques, can be provided by solving feature selection and parameter optimization issues. The researchers assert that feature selection could be enhanced by recursive feature elimination. Additionally, results of the study indicate that parameter optimization was solved in practice by using the application of a grid-search algorithm. This grid-search algorithm was shown to select the model parameters, which subsequently set the range for higher accuracy. The researchers conclude that SVM prediction accuracy improvements could be demonstrated through optimized parameters, thus improving the prediction rate of hard landings.

Ju and Tian (2012) introduce knowledge-based SVM via nearest points (NPKBSVM), to address the context of prior knowledge in SVMs. Their research indicates that SVMs can play a significant role in data mining methods. They continue to assert that the construction of hyperplanes can be used for classification and regression, among other tasks. Their research describes that, regarding classification problems, increased separation can be accomplished by the hyperplane, which lowers the generalization error of the classifier by increasing the margins. Concurrently, they build on the work of Lauer and Bloch (2008) with the introduction of the kernel function, which addresses non-linearity. They also indicate that several methods of SVMs will continue to emerge because of demands, which will allow SVMs to solve problems efficiently and effectively.

Chidambaram and Srinivasagan (2018), *Ju and Tian (2012)*, and *Lauer and Bloch (2008)* agree that prior knowledge and non-linear sets can be integrated into SVMs as linear constraints. The researchers also claim that this can lead to optimization challenges that necessitate the use of sophisticated convex optimization tools. Incorporating the use of prior knowledge into the computation process of shortest distance as measured from difference in the training data points and the knowledge sets produces an amended set of training data. The researchers conclude that current SVM tools can be used to achieve significantly improved optimization levels using prior knowledge advantages.

Pressing On

Lauer and Bloch (2008) summarize how the integration of prior knowledge into SVMs can be crucial in order to enhance the performance of SVMs in many applications. The researchers provide a review of studies that utilizes the two general types of prior knowledge into classification tasks: *class-invariance and knowledge on the data*. The former describes transformation invariances in domains of input space, and the latter contains knowledge on the quality of the data or accuracy issues in the training data set. Lauer and Bloch (2008) review the uses of prior knowledge with a brief description:

> *Prior knowledge refers to all information about the problem available in addition to the training data. Several classifiers incorporate the smoothness assumption that a test pattern similar to one of the training samples tends to be assigned to the same class. Also, choosing the soft-margin version of SVMs can be seen as a use of prior knowledge on the non-divisibility of the data or the presence of outliers and noise in the training set. However, in both cases, these assumptions are intrinsically made by the SV learning and are thus excluded from the definition of prior knowledge. In machine learning, the importance of prior knowledge can be seen from the no free lunch theorem, which states that all the algorithms perform the same when averaged over the different problems. Thus, it implies that to gain in performance one must use a specialized algorithm that includes some prior knowledge about the problem at hand. (p. 1,581)*

Key contributions of Lauer and Bloch (2008) to the literature include their conclusions that the inclusion of prior knowledge via SME input expert knowledge can improve future SVM model performance. The researchers go on to assert that this in turn could also improve classification performance, thus enhanced practical implications. They recommend continued research in order to explore other forms of prior knowledge, together with optimized algorithms for their implementations. The researchers also describe how the combination of different types of knowledge might be explored for practical applications.

Finally, *Mendes (2012)* builds on the research regarding SVM methods with his study on anomaly detection using ML classifiers exploring flight data. The researcher used SVM techniques to investigate automatic landings in A320 aircraft over a period of two months, exploring 359 flight events. Specifically, the researcher investigated how both classification models can predict both normal and abnormal flight characteristics of an aircraft autoland system as determined through the analysis of flight data. The research uses exceedance-based criteria set by the aircraft manufacturer then explores the use of algorithms to detect atypical or outlier values. The study details how this approach allows the detection of those situations in an unsupervised learning environment, thus increasing efficiency.

Important results of the study include the finding that principal component analysis (PCA) improved the correlation between dimensions. A linear relationship between the features was enhanced through the reduction of variance, thus leading to an increased anomaly detection rate. The researcher also recommended that future research be conducted into the cases that PCA detected, in addition to the detected SVM cases. The researcher concluded that PCA and SVM, when used in combination, provided an optimized solution regarding the final case labels. Finally, the study indicates that a collaboration of these methods allows robust detection improvement.

Random forest

Sometimes referred to as random decision forests, RFs are another example of machine learning techniques using ensemble learning methods for regression and classification. They operate by building numerous decision trees in the data training phase of the AVSKD data processing model. Advantages of RFs include the ability to mitigate the tendency of decision trees of overfitting their training data set. Breiman (2001) describes the construction of numerous, unrelated decision trees using the Classification and Regression Tree (CART) model. CART was developed by Breiman with trees for both classification and regression purposes. The basic premise of CART is that the product of the process is the determination of where to split the trees, using ensemble methods to accomplish the construction of multiple trees. Breiman introduces RFs as a classifier focusing on bootstrap aggregating, which constructs the trees by iteratively sampling the training data set, and eventually forming a consensus predictive value Breiman (1999). Breiman asserts that one of the advantages of this bootstrapping technique is better model performance, achieved by decreasing model variance, while not allowing an increase in the bias. Breiman continues to describe another advantage of bootstrapping as a way of addressing correlation issues with similar trees, achieved by using sampling strategies from different training sets (Breiman, 2001). RFs are distinguishable from bagging in that RFs create a random subset during feature selection, thus identifying strong features regarding prediction of the target variable indicating strength of correlation among predictor and target variables.

Mathews et al. (2013) detail several challenges in the AVSKD data processing model, particularly those challenges dealing with missing values. They provide research indicating that missing values are often a significant factor in the examination of FDM data. Hapfelmeier and Ulm (2014) provide research on mitigation strategies when considering missing data in RF model development. The researchers detail variable selection strategies when considering missing values. They suggest that RFs could be utilized in the variable selection process to enhance data analysis and predictive accuracy. The researchers continue to suggest that several solution strategies could be used to address missing values: multiple imputation, case analysis, and a significance metric. Results of their study indicate that RFs achieve the best results with a self-contained metric in selecting relevant variables regarding the predictive model construction. The researchers conclude that when data contains missing predictor values, measures like multiple imputation or self-contained metrics could be used. The researchers recommend that when using RF modeling with missing values, self-contained metrics can be used successfully to select variables which are of relevance for prediction.

Paul and Dupont (2015) build on the work on Breiman (1999, 2001) with their study on statistically significant feature selection problems. The team presents the results of experiments using RFs to demonstrate how these modelling techniques can address problems associated with feature selection of predictor variables. The researchers assert that RFs can be used to analyze embedded variables selected in the feature selection process. They propose a statistical process in order to measure variable importance regarding significance in the interaction with other variables in RFs. Results of the study demonstrate the correct identification of relevant variables, using Breiman's index of importance (Breiman, 2001). Significant results of the study include the ability to calculate p-values during the iterative RF model building process. In this way, the researchers detail how to discover significant predictor values while minimizing false identification. The researchers conclude that the RF predictive modelling processes consistently perform better than other modelling techniques, without sacrificing performance.

Genuer, Poggi, Tuleau-Malot, and Villa-Vialaneix (2017) and *Singh, Gupta, Sevakula, and Verma (2016)* conducted research comparing RFs with other ML algorithms, as applied to very large data. Genuer et al (2017) investigated and compared the performance of several ensemble ML techniques, such as linear regression models, clustering methods and bootstrapping schemes. The researchers build upon theories presented by Breiman (2001), who introduced RFs as decision trees integrated with aggregation and bootstrap ideas, which are effective regarding the consideration of regression problems and two-class as well as multi-class classification analysis. Genuer et al. (2017) also compare and contrast several variants of RF modeling algorithms on datasets consisting of 120 million observations. Variations in the modeling include parallel implementation, several different forms of bootstrapping, and various subsampling techniques. Additionally, Genuer et al. (2017) included a sample experiment detailing the application to real-world data related to flight delays. These data were used mainly for descriptive purposes rather than aviation research.

Singh et al. (2016) contrast this approach, while focusing on Gaussian mixture model (GMM), logistic regression, and RF classifiers used in mining large data. The researchers analyzed these algorithms while comparing run time, test accuracy, and number of mappers on large data sets. The study focused on three big data sets comprised of over two million sets of data. Results of the study detail RFs perform best in terms of accuracy. Although Genuer et al. (2017) also assert that RFs perform best when trees are diversified, the researchers recommend that improvement in RF performance should be attained when improvements regarding diversity are defined in initial RF iterations.

Lee, Park, and Jung (2014) describe aviation research using RFs and similarity measures to build predictive models that determine aircraft system fault detection. The researchers conducted research on unmanned aircraft vehicle (UAV) fault detection systems using a fault detection algorithm they developed. Fault decision was conducted with the calculation of prioritized similarity measure. The impact of predictor variables was determined and weighted using RFs. The researchers identified 89 data variables in feature selection, 39 being variables associated with normal operations, and 51 variables detailing non-normal flight conditions. Prior knowledge and familiarity with the data were used as factors in the determination of impact variables.

The fault detection models were built using both lateral and longitudinal flight control surface related variables. Results achieved with the performance of RFs indicate the impact of each feature or parameter. Several flight tests were conducted in order to validate the fault detection models. Significant results of the study include the demonstration of the feasibility of fault detection algorithm using RFs. Additionally, high fault detection rates were observed, as well as the validation of similarity measure decision results. The researchers note that the flight control system of the UAV could be enhanced without the requirement of additional sensors, thus saving aircraft weight and complexity.

Gregorutti, Michel, and Saint-Pierre (2015) propose a new approach to the use of RFs, with emphasis on multiple Functional Data Analysis (FDA) and the grouped variable importance measure, used in their study to predict aircraft landing distance. The researchers assert that several groupings of basis coefficients could be utilized considering specific functional disposition. Unique to the research model is the approach to the selection RF algorithm, when considering the grouped variable importance. The computational requirements of the RF algorithm were decreased by regrouping the coefficients, which contrasts to the iterative elimination of grouping coefficients usually demonstrated in RF modeling by eliminating one coefficient in each iteration. The team also describe how simulation studies demonstrate scale of the grouped importance regarding measurement for FDA.

The research team then applied the resulting RF algorithm in the feature selection of important factors in long landings to explore and predict aircraft landing distances. The team consulted with several SMEs, who determined that 23 variables were relevant to landing distance. 1868 flights were used, operating at one airport by one airline, to collect data. RFs as well as a permutation-based importance measures were used for variable groupings. The researchers also compared and assessed models using bagging, neural network, and SVM ML techniques. Key contributions of the study include the unique application the team used to select operational variables using the measure of grouped variable importance and a predictive modeling approach. Additionally, the RFs were adapted in a backward context regarding iterative elimination. This variable selection technique was also adapted to the unique measure of grouped importance in order to predict the target variable, landing distance. The researchers conclude that future studies could incorporate their group variable importance projection technique into flight data analysis to assist airline flight training managers to develop SOPs as well as enhance pilot training.

Blair, Lee, and Davies (2017) use RFs to build models used by aircraft to detect real time inflight aircraft damage. The researchers developed techniques for detection using real-time classification of flight trajectories distinguishing normal from abnormal aircraft. The team demonstrated an efficient computational approach using RFs, with the key factor being the ability to provide accuracy necessary for fault detection and classification. The methods were tested using a full motion 757 flight simulator at the NASA ARC research center. The team used RFs in their approach to detect fault in six flight scenarios in the simulator. Principal Component Analysis (PCA) was used in the classification study as a dimension reduction technique. The chosen methodology integrated several statistical techniques: principal component analysis, random forest, and cross-validation, which the team asserts produced a reliable and fast classifier. The team then used sliding window approach, which the team describes as a sequential approach to the problem, while concurrently learning temporal and probability thresholds, by training a validation data set. The team claims their methods resulted in a

98.7% predictive accuracy rate, and also provided fault detection at half-second time intervals. This key result from the study indicates that faster fault detection times could be achieved with increased computational capabilities, which would ultimately assist the pilot in real-time SA enhancement.

Tong, Yin, Wang, and Zheng (2018) analyze and process QAR using RFs to predict the landing speed of commercial aircraft. The researchers collected data from the QAR devices onboard Airbus 300 aircraft from a single operator based on 2000 flight segments. The team asserts that missing data was a significant challenge in the data processing task. In order to address this challenge, the researchers resampled the data at one frame per second. The team then used RFs to sort the 69 candidate features in order of importance and selected the 20 most relevant features regarding landing speed. The RF process resulted in 250 trees determining the top 20 features. Top features included engine speed (thrust), angle of attack, and descent rate. The research team asserts that their most significant result was the ability to predict landing speed, which they describe as a causal factor in landing accidents. Additionally, the team describes how RFs were able to extract the most important features. The team recommends that AI be incorporated into future studies in order to process the sensor data.

Lv, Yu, and Zhu (2018) provide research into hazards associated with RE based on excessive landing distance. The researchers used SVM, RF, and logistic modeling of QAR data from 6,000 Chinese Airlines A320 flights. The researchers present results that indicate excessively long landings are significantly correlated with pilot flare technique and runway distance. Limitations in the study include lack of standards applied in the feature selection phase of the knowledge discovery process as well as the lack of SME involvement in the selection of impact variables.

Finally, Kumar and Ghosh (2019) detail the use of CART and RFs in their research into predicting unsteady aerodynamics model using quasi-stall flight test data. The researchers assert that RFs were more effective regarding scalability than NN models. The team developed RFs model specifically to model lift, drag, and pitching moment aerodynamic models. The team chose to use non-parametric models using the flight data. They describe that non-parametric models do not include physical parameters or parametric equations like parametric models do. The team presents CART and RF data-driven modeling approaches by understanding the gathered flight data and using this prior knowledge in feature selection.

The researchers agree that advantages of RFs include avoiding overfitting problems often encountered by decision tree, diversity regarding both classification and regression, and important predictor identification based on training data. Results compared favorably with maximum likelihood estimation (MLE) predictions. The team declare that the key conclusion in the study was that RFs are superior to CART, with each method more desirable alternative to the parametric approach inherent in MLE. The team states that RFs could be scaled and applied to many other applications of nonlinear modeling.

Gradient boost machine

One of several recently developed machine learning algorithm-based techniques, gradient boost machines (GBMs) are used mainly for classification and regression. The product of this technique is prediction models formed by integrating weaker prediction models, usually decision tree. GBMs typically build the model in an iterative process. Additionally, GBMs are able to generalize the integration of the weaker individual models, which can produce an optimized differential loss function (Breiman, 1997). Breiman (1997) and Freidman (2001) developed early gradient boosting optimization algorithms, mainly based on cost analysis.

Friedman (2001) continued research using optimization algorithms, conducting significant research on algorithms expressly for work on regression using gradient boosting. Although his research initially observed boosting algorithms that optimized cost functions over function space, this functional perspective of gradient boosting preceded development of boosting algorithms in many areas of ML, including aviation research exceeding classification and regression. GBMs integrate multiple weak models into one strong model, with the purpose of predicting a target variable probability using supervised learning. A training data set is typically used to teach a model to predict the target variable in an iterative process that can minimize the mean squared error, for example, in a regression problem. The iterative process continues to improve as the error is minimized in each iteration and produces a residual, which is a negative gradient. In effect, GBMs incorporate the negative residual into the next iteration.

Similar to other supervised learning problems, GBMs produce an output variable and a vector of input variables. The vector, or joint probability distribution, uses the training data set to develop a function in order to minimize loss. The work of Breiman and Friedman has provided aviation researchers with foundational tools to investigate and explore problems associated with predictive model construction using GBMs. A brief description of extant literature pertaining to GBM techniques, as applied to aviation, is provided. To date, the general area of research has been accomplished concerning cost savings and optimization, with some work done on flight path prediction.

Alligier and Gianazza (2018) provide aviation research using GBMs to build predictive models focusing on ground-based aircraft trajectory. Their research models the forces imposed on an aircraft to predict future points of the trajectory of the flight path. They assert that previous knowledge was necessary regarding aircraft mass, thrust, and speed. The researchers applied ML methods in order build models to predict mass and speed as constructs, thus improving the ability to predict their target variable, aircraft trajectory. The data used in the research was provided by the Eurocontrol Base of Aircraft Data (BADA), which was utilized to provide default values for the model parameters. The data were acquired on ADS-B from The OpenSky Network in 2017, using the climbing segments of 11 types of aircraft, resulting in millions of flights worldwide, operating from 1520 airports.

The ML techniques were used to predict the most significant factors necessary to calculate the predicted trajectory. The researchers used GBMs to build predictive models for each specific aircraft type. As mentioned, previous knowledge was then required to construct a training data set, with known operational factors. The training set was constructed by separating, or partitioning, the original large set of data. The researchers claim that they achieved two of their stated goals: a non-optimistically biased result, and the demonstration of the use of explanatory, real-time variables in a performance assessment.

Significant contributions to the body of knowledge were achieved regarding bias: the climbing segments were not limited by altitude restrictions, and very large data were included in the study, using millions of climbing segments of the 11 most popular aircraft types in commercial aviation. Thus, the researchers demonstrated that ML techniques can be effectively scaled to very large data. The researchers detail that further significant practical implications apply to air traffic control, which could benefit from the results of the study, regarding the ability to predict climb trajectory and vertical separation. Additionally, the ability to predict climb trajectory real-time could enhance flight path track error and improve top of climb prediction.

Research by *Thompson (2017)* using FAA Comprehensive Electronic Data Analysis and Reporting (CEDAR) data provides an example of the use of ADS-B data in modeling unstable approaches. Thompson (2017) asserts that ADS-B data could be augmented with weather observation data for development of real-time stable approach models. The researcher asserts that these real-time models could be used by air traffic control to calculate the probability of occurrence of an unstable approach and rejected landing. Thompson (2017) also indicates that the capability for ATC to predict an unstable approach and rejected landing could improve safety by decreasing interference with air traffic flow in normal operations. The researchers concur that the ability to predict the occurrence of rejected landings improves air traffic safety. Alligier and Gianazza (2018) and Thompson (2017) agree that future work should include analysis of specific airport operations, at which error in prediction was higher, in order to help improve unstable approach model accuracy.

Achenbach and Spinler (2018) introduce ensemble modeling, combining elements of linear regression and GBM algorithms to generate predictive models. The researchers provide airline arrival time and cost index optimization predictions on European airspace short haul flights. Cost index (CI) is an airline metric used to predict fuel cost and flight time of a flight segment. The researchers describe the cost savings airlines can attain through accurate flight planning based on CI predictive accuracy. The researchers assert that increased efforts by aviation researchers to minimize costs associated with flight delays have faced challenges due to inability to accurately combine arrival time predictions with CI models. Contrasting previous studies, the researchers chose to use a ML ensemble to predict arrival time, but rather than predicting arrival time once the aircraft was airborne, they chose to use gate departure to predict arrival time.

Achenbach and Spinler (2018) continue to build on the work of Breiman (1997) and Friedman (2001) using GBMs based on European flight data from 2015 and 2016, from over 200 European airports. The researchers identified important predictor variables regarding weather data, airport congestion, flight levels, and other basic flight planning data. The predictive modeling then focused on arrival time with various CI values. Significant contributions of their study include the first attempt to combine dynamic CI values with arrival time predictions. This combination produced greatly improved ability to airline managers to minimize total cost of a flight segment. Additionally, the study demonstrated the increase in accuracy by using ensemble GBMs. These key contributions provide evidence that ensemble GBMs can improve aircraft arrival time predictions while considering both linear and non-linear relationships of important impact variables, along with the interdependence of these variables. Limitations to the study are that it focused on one airline. The researchers recommend future research include several airlines, in order to apply their model to airlines of different sizes and city pairs. Additionally, CI was calculated based on cost per unit of time, when in reality, often cost of time cannot be determined per minute for all variables. Lack of enroute weather conditions, including wind effects, was a delimitation of the study, and could significantly affect results. Regarding future research, they recommend that extensions of their work include improved cost estimates for not only delays but also cost per unit time be further investigated. The researchers assert that ML techniques should be incorporated with predictive modeling in future studies with the ability to combine cost blocks in order to improve CI optimization.

Kang and Hansen (2018) build on the work of Achenbach and Spinler (2018) with their research on the application of GBMs to improve commercial airline fuel burn prediction. The researchers built predictive models using prediction intervals (PIs) to mitigate the uncertainty of model predictions. The researchers determined that annual cost savings to airlines could approximate $60 million annually, just for one domestic US airline. Additional benefits include the reduction by 428 million kg of CO_2 annually per airline. Data for the study were collected from three sources: flight level performance data from the FAA Aviation System Performance Metrics (APSM) database, the terminal area forecast (TAF) weather information from the National Oceanic and Atmospheric Administration (NOAA) database and flight and fuel statistics from one U.S. airline.

The researchers included all available predictive variables to build the models. The target variable for their study was actual fuel burn for a flight segment. The FAA ASPM database was used to gather historical data for the largest 77 US airports, then descriptive statistics were generated to create flight time data between different city pairs. The researchers then describe the various advantages that advanced computing power and new ML techniques have allowed. They describe GBMs with the ability to iteratively improve predictive accuracy by starting with a weak learner base, then continuously adding them together.

The researchers contrast GBM ML techniques with other ensemble learning methods such as Bagging, Random Forest, and Stacking. Similar to Achenbach and Spinler (2018), the researchers determined that a significant limitation to their study was the lack of real-time enroute weather data. They assert that current data made available by the airlines is based on the flight planning system (FPS), which is subject to prediction errors, which could significantly affect fuel burn values. The researchers recommend, in future studies, the investigation of predictive model construction, focusing on airline dispatcher decision making. The researchers detail the affects that human decision-making processes could have on the fuel planning process, and raise the question of HIP and ADM regarding predictive model applications.

Finally, *Gallego, Gómez, Sáez, Orenga, and Valdés (2018)* produced research with the objective of investigating the effects of operational input variables on the vertical flight path trajectory prediction. Additionally, the research team desired to determine what important input variables should be included in the feature selection segment of the knowledge discovery process. The study was based on the use of a data warehouse (DWH) program to construct a comprehensive information management layer. The aircraft trajectory flow models were based on these data, applied to the Barcelona International Airport. ML techniques were used to determine the flow patterns within the DWH. Contrasting other similar studies, the researchers chose to use a set of multilevel linear models (MLMs) which were adopted to investigate vertical aircraft flight path trajectories on descent into the airport. Key discriminators included operational vertical procedures, airline specific procedures, and unique flow patterns to the airport.

The MLMs performed linear regression tasks, which included training the independent variables for different groups. The target variable was the rate of descent from the top of descent (TOD) to Flight Level 250. The researchers indicate that results show a correlation between rate of descent and the location of the TOD. The researchers continue to conclude that based on the MLM results, key input variables were determined to be the position of TOD and flow factor, regarding flight path trajectory prediction.

Additionally, specific airline operational procedures (SOPs) were not found to be significant factors in the prediction of flight path trajectory. The researchers recommend that future research investigate different airspace sectors for flow similarities. The researchers also agree with Kang and Hansen (2018) and Achenbach and Spinler (2018) that future research should incorporate weather-related data for improving accuracy of the predictive models. Finally, the researchers recommend that GBMs, as well as other data-driven approaches, should be explored in order to more accurately predict aircraft flight path trajectory.

Unanswered Questions in Aviation Research

A review of the extant aviation research literature on topics pertinent to the study was conducted. The three areas of focus were: (a) federal guidelines and oversight of hazards associated with unstable approaches and runway excursions, (b) aviation research conducted on pilot risk perception and risk tolerance, and (c) aviation research using predictive modelling based on advanced ML techniques applied to large FDR data. While the review describes many examples of aviation research in each of these topics, the recommendations among the aviation researchers conducting the most recent relevant work (approximately last five years) describes gaps and opportunities for future research and is presented here.

Unstable approach and runway excursion hazards. The FAA, NTSB, and FSF have provided oversight, guidance, and/or recommendations to operators regarding the hazards associated with mitigating the risk of runway excursions. The FAA has listed unstable approaches as one of the most common causal factors (FAA, 2014). The FSF and NTSB corroborate this assertion that stable approaches (and safe landings) begin early in the approach planning phase of flight (FSF, 2009; NTSB, 2016, 2019b). These organizations have called for improved pilot training initiatives, enhanced CRM training, as well as research into risk mitigation strategies for operators to avoid the hazards associated with unstable approaches (FAA, 2017b; NTSB, 2016, 2019b). Recent aviation accidents have demonstrated that unstable approaches continue to be causal factors. The NTSB has recommended that the aviation industry respond to the hazard of unstable approaches with improvements in pilot training, as well as the development of CRM techniques to enhance pilot risk assessment and perception in flight operations (NTSB, 2013, 2019b).

Pilot risk perception and risk tolerance. You and Han (2013) describe how the safe operational behavior of pilots can be affected by HF characteristics such as ADM, HIP, SA, and interpersonal communications and teamwork attitudes. The researchers build on the previous work of Hunter (2005) regarding the correlation between pilot risk perception and hazardous events.

They used the Risk Perception Scale developed by Hunter to conduct surveys of pilot attitudes associated with perception of risk and the relative levels of safety inherent in airline operations. Results of the study indicate that present research on pilot risk perception and risk tolerance vary with pilot perception of locus of control, or the belief that one has a direct effect of the outcome of a situation. The researchers continue to assert that once a pilot achieves a certain threshold of flight experience, measured in total flight time, then perception of internal locus of control diminishes. Important recommendations for future research regarding pilot risk perception are that future research be conducted to identify key factors that contribute to inaccurate perceptions of risk, as well as the exploration of effects of organizational safety culture on safe operational behaviors.

Ju, Ji, Lan, and You (2017) conducted research addressing recommendations by You and Han (2013) by investigating what factors affect pilot perception of risk. Specifically, the study explored the relationship between narcissistic personality and optimism in aviation risk perception. A key component of the research was to determine whether self-promotion mediated the personality traits of narcissism and over-optimism in pilot risk perception. Results of the study indicated that narcissism had a significant effect on risk perception among pilots, in that overestimation of promotion focus predicts underestimation of risk. The researchers limited their study to that of optimism bias and recommend that future studies address other cognitive biases. The research team also recommends that active airline pilots be included in the study, rather than the inclusion of only flight students. Agreeing with You and Han (2013), the researcher concurs that organizational safety culture effects on pilot risk perception be explored.

Predictive modeling using recorded flight data. The literature provides several examples of research based on anomaly detection to identify abnormal flight events. Bharadwaj et al. (2013) detail a multifaceted process of discovering and describing unusual events as Anomaly Detection. They use the term synonymously with unusual occurrences, outliers, and surprises. The researchers further assert that the process encompasses several attributes, including the type of anomaly, the nature of the data, and the handling of uncertainty inherent in the system. Contextual anomalies describe abnormal occurrences as defined by guidelines or expectations. For example, an unstable approach is considered an anomaly in the context of this research, as defined by any exceedance of limitations presented in FAA AC 120-71A and later refined in AC 91-79A. Hence, anomaly detection can be described as occurrences that do not fall into normal regions of expectations or standards. In terms of complex systems with multiple regions of normal behaviors, such as flight operations (takeoff, cruise, descent, and approach and landing phases of flight), anomaly detection describes operations which do not fall into these regions. The researchers further assert that abnormal behaviors may appear as clusters that are discernible from normal clusters. Thus, these clusters can become the framework which describes clustering algorithms models.

Building upon this work, *Li et al. (2015)* and *Aslaner, Unal, and Iyigun (2016)* applied clustering techniques to flight data to identify anomalies in the takeoff and landing phases of flight. The research was designed using two experimental methods: one to sample 91 flight parameters in the effort to identify abnormal flight events and a second to evaluate three different data clustering algorithms. Limitations to the study include a vague description of what constitutes abnormal flight events, variables of interest in the clustering analysis, and the lack of a clearly defined target variable. It is also unclear what coding was used to build the models used in the evaluation of the algorithms. Additionally, the SMEs used in the evaluation of the abnormal flight events do not apply any standard criteria in their analysis. The researchers agree that future research should investigate the application of advanced ML techniques to large FDM data to try and identify previously unknown anomalies.

Gera and Goel (2015) suggest that data mining is part of a more general process based on the discovery of knowledge pertaining to large data. They further describe the idea that several sources of data can be exploited simultaneously and introduce the concept of dynamic and static sources of data. Dynamic data sets, like those generated by FDR data of commercial aircraft operations in the NAS, are particularly important to aviation research. The research team recommends that future research use large FDM data to explore the continuously changing environmental conditions inherent in the NAS.

Tong et al. (2018) analyze and process QAR using RFs to predict the landing speed of commercial aircraft. The researchers collected data from the QAR devices onboard Airbus A300 aircraft from a single operator based on 2000 flight segments. The research team asserts that their most significant result was the ability to predict landing speed, which they describe as a causal factor in landing accidents. Additionally, the team describes how RFs were able to extract the most important features. The team recommends that AI be incorporated into future studies in order to process the sensor data.

Gallego et al. (2018) produced research with the objective of investigating the effects of operational input variables on the vertical flight path trajectory prediction. Additionally, the research team desired to determine what important input variables should be included in the feature selection segment of the knowledge discovery process. ML techniques were used to determine the flow patterns within the DWH. Contrasting other similar studies, the researchers chose to use a set of Multilevel Linear Models (MLMs), which were adopted to investigate vertical aircraft flight path trajectories on descent into the airport. Key discriminators included: operational vertical procedures, airline specific procedures, and unique flow patterns to the airport. The researchers recommend that future research investigate different airspace sectors for flow similarities. The researchers also agree with Kang and Hansen (2018) and Achenbach and Spinler (2018) that future research should incorporate weather-related data for improving accuracy of the predictive models. Finally, the researchers recommend that GBMs, as well as other data-driven approaches, should be explored in order to more accurately predict aircraft flight path trajectory.

Finally, *Oehling and Barry (2019)* present the use of ML techniques to detect unknown occurrences in flight data, generated by approximately three hundred aircraft, from six different Airbus A320 fleets and sub-fleets, for over 1000 flights per day, from March 2013 to March 2016. The researchers introduce methods enhancing the safety knowledge discovery process. They continue to describe ML in terms of algorithms which learn from the data. The researchers assert that effective uses have been demonstrated with software which builds models, based on input data, rather than a predefined model which was encoded in the software during algorithm development. The study divides ML subcategories into both supervised and unsupervised learning. Supporting the recommendations of Aslaner et al. (2016), Bharadwaj et al. (2013), and Li et al. (2015), the researchers recommend that future studies using advanced ML methods be applied to large FDM data to detect unknown anomalies.

Walker (2017) details the development of the modern QAR. The ability to gather large FDM data with advances in QAR technology has encouraged new developments in advanced data driven techniques such as advanced ML methods. The large data being gathered daily in the NAS by these QAR devices has presented an opportunity for the exploration and investigation of these data. Aviation research using data mining of QAR data has progressed from strictly exceedance-based anomaly detection, to both semi-supervised and unsupervised ML methods. The researcher makes an important assertion regarding the concept of leading vs. lagging indications of measurable precursors to accidents or incidents. Walker makes the distinction between reactive discovery based on lagging indicators and proactive discovery based on leading indicators. This distinction is significant regarding the transition from reactive to predictive modeling of flight data. Walker continues to describe the evolution of the use of flight data collection devices from post-accident analysis to actively accessing, analyzing, and preventing anomalous flight events.

Das et al. (2010) conducted research using known exceedance criteria and applied the criteria to QAR data using MKAD and CAD to detect anomalous events on commercial aircraft. The data driven study compared several different ML algorithms to detect previously unknown anomalous events. Similar to the study conducted by Li et al. (2016), a structured process was not used in the cleaning, examination, or processing of the FDM data. In both of these cases, SMEs were used to design exceedance criteria, which were then used to identify variables of interest, prior to the application of cluster analysis-based ML techniques. These works focused on the identification of anomalous events, as defined by SMEs, rather than a standardized aviation knowledge discovery process based on industry standard or federal guidelines.

Bharadwaj et al. (2013) led a NASA Aviation Safety project to develop data driven, supervised and unsupervised techniques to enhance the diagnostic capabilities of in-flight systems' reasoners. The researchers build on the work of Li et al. (2016) and Das et al. (2010) using supervised clustering techniques to detect anomalous events. The team advances the data process model with a data driven analysis using feature analysis based on nominal data frame comparison. Similar to previous works, the research is limited by the necessity of SME developed exceedance criteria.

Summary

Although hazards have been identified with the continued occurrences of runway excursions, a reliable and valid representation of rejected landing decision-making based on unstable approach criteria has not been fully investigated (Koteeswaran et al., 2017). Limitations inherent in qualitative methods are evident in the literature, with examples of text mining narratives from LOSA field observations, NASA voluntary ASRS reports, and surveys. The extant literature does not indicate that there is research that addresses or exploits the large amount of aircraft data available (Matthews et al., 2013). Recent studies have described that aviation researchers have begun to realize the application of advanced data mining techniques as an appropriate and powerful tool to handle these voluminous data being generated daily by FDM and FOQA programs (Li et al., 2015; Puranik & Mavris, 2018; Shi et al., 2017). However, these recent studies have focused primarily on the validation and evaluation of advanced mathematical algorithms and leave analysis of safety mitigation information for either further research or with the qualitative assessment of a subject matter expert (Arockia et al., 2016; Li et al., 2015; Puranik, & Mavris, 2018).

Finally, several salient aspects of the literature become evident based on the review focusing on large data and prediction of in-flight anomalies. The first factor that becomes apparent is the large amount of data that are being recorded by advanced digital flight recorders on every commercial airline flight in the NAS. Airlines are encouraged by the FAA to voluntarily participate in the FOQA program. FOQA was designed to improve safety in commercial aviation by allowing airlines and pilots to share de-identified aggregate information with the FAA so that the

FAA can monitor national trends in aircraft operations and focus its resources to address risk issues (e.g., flight operations, air traffic control (ATC), airports) (FAA, 2004).

Although voluntary (in the United States), the FOQA program has resulted in very large amounts of flight data that have not been accessed on a scale appropriate for these data. Even though pilot safety reports, accident reports, and safety debrief narratives constitute a large amount of data, the literature indicates that these data have only been explored with the use of text mining and qualitative methods. Second, while a review of the literature indicates that various statistical analytical methods have revealed clear patterns in the prediction of pilot performance, these data have not been exploited in order to fully investigate significant relationships of the predictors. Third, the extant literature indicates that once the relationship connecting pilot performance to flight anomaly variable inputs was explained, that future pilot performance in the approach and landing phases of flight could be estimated. Finally, although much of the existing literature presents results on the evaluation of complex algorithms applied to large data, subject matter experts have been required to analyze the results and apply them to aviation problems. A review of the existing literature indicates a gap in the research in the application of predictive modeling techniques, particularly the application of these techniques to the prediction of probability of occurrence of factors contributing to pilot misperception of risk.

MOVING FORWARD

While the identification of the phenomenon labeled as UARM in this study was a straight forward process, FOQA data indicate that the problem of pilots pressing on continues to exist. Pilot lapses in risk perception include the idea that stable approach criteria can be exceeded and still press on to safe landings. Current FOQA data are consistent in the revelation that approximately 95% of unstable approaches are continued to landing attempts. Pilot assessment of stable approach criteria at 500 feet AGL lends to the idea that continuation bias to a landing attempt is very difficult for the line pilot to resist. Once the pilot has flown the approach to 500 feet AGL, a rejected landing is a wake-up call that rarely occurs.

What can be done to prevent the occurrence of UARM? I believe, in part, the answer is that existing pilot alerting technologies should be incorporated into the modern flight deck the same way takeoff configuration warning alerting systems and GPWS warning systems have been. I propose that the complex assessment process pilots must perform while already mentally committed to landing be replaced, or at least augmented, with flight deck alerting technology that would provide a warning and thus, making the concept of continuing an unstable approach to landing very difficult for a pilot to accept. Similar to landing configuration warnings, the UARM alert could provide the impetus for pilots to reject the temptation of continuation bias associated with pressing on to a landing attempt during an unstable approach.

Pressing On

Consider for a moment if the pilots of Asiana 214 were faced with an aural alert and a visual warning at 500 feet AGL on the approach to runway 28L at the San Francisco International airport in July 2013. My assertion is that no matter what had previously transpired to place the aircrew in this particular predicament, the accident could have been prevented had an alerting system provided the pilots with undeniable evidence that a landing was not safe or desired, and that a rejected landing was the best and most prudent course of action. Pilots can be trained to react positively and decisively to warning and alerting systems. My assertion is that an AI-based unstable approach alerting system warning the pilots of an unstable approach would help to successfully mitigate the risk associated with UARM.

New flight deck technologies are already in development that could be used to perform these tasks. Honeywell's SmartLanding™ system is one such system that alerts aircrew when the aircraft exceeds certain stable approach criteria. New systems such as SmartLanding™ would not produce an aural or visual advisory under normal stable approach conditions, but would issue both aural and visual advisories/cautions in the case of an unstable approach. Once integrated into modern flight deck design, these new systems could be incorporated into pilot simulator training scenarios. The combination of new flight deck technology alerting systems and enhanced aircrew training would help to successfully address safety risk mitigation strategies regarding the human performance issues associated with continuation bias and unstable approaches.

Will solely incorporating new flight deck technology and unstable approach warning systems into transport aircraft be sufficient to mitigate the risk associated with UARM? As we have discovered with accidents such as Asiana 214 and PK 8303, automation and flight deck alerting technologies alone are not sufficient to always break the chain of events causing an accident or incident. Pilots of PK 8303 were reported to have continued an unstable approach with both aural and visual warning cues provided by both GPWS and landing gear configuration alerting systems. It is logical to deduce that adding another warning system, such as I have suggested, would not solely provide the impetus for the crew to identify the unstable approach and perform a rejected landing.

Governmental regulatory guidance, air carrier standard operating procedures, and an increased emphasis on pilot monitoring duties have all had some level of success in improving unstable approach risk mitigation strategies, however, the data from FSF, FAA, IATA, and in my research, all corroborate the fact that approximately 95% of unstable approaches do not result in the desired outcome, a rejected landing. Fortunately, most of these instances of UARM have not proven to be catastrophic. However, accidents such as Asiana 214 and PK 8303 provide ample evidence of a persistence of this aviation problem that shows no indications of disappearing.

Industry, governmental aviation agencies, and academia have consistently emphasized the importance of addressing unstable approaches and the risk of runway excursions and/or collision with terrain with little consequence. The conclusions and recommendations based on my research not only demonstrate the scope of the aviation problem, but also several salient solutions. A combination of (a) new pilot alerting technologies, (b) enhanced aircrew simulator training, and (c) integration of (a) and (b) into air carrier SRM would give pilots not only the training and education on how to avoid UARM, but also the awareness regarding the level of unacceptable risk associated with continuing to a landing attempt when faced with evidence of an unstable approach.

APPENDIX

Research Methodology

The research methodology was modelled after that introduced by Matthews et al. (2013), the aviation safety knowledge discovery (AVSKD) process. The AVSKD process describes the entire process for analyzing aviation data from raw FOQA data to reporting of predictive models. The AVSKD framework illustrated in Figure 5 was adapted as the framework for the methodology for the research.

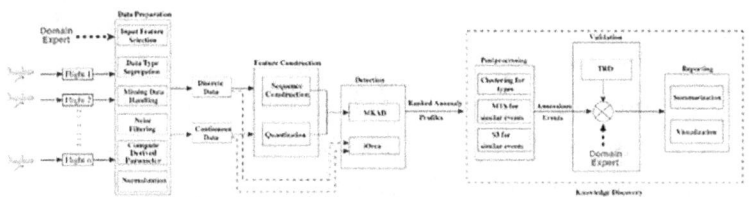

Figure 5. Aviation safety knowledge discovery (AVSKD) process. From "Discovering Anomalous Aviation Safety Events Using Scalable Data Mining Algorithms," by B. Matthews, S. Das, K. Bhaduri, K. Das, R. Martin, and N. Oza, 2013, Journal of Aerospace Information Systems, 10(10), p. 469. Copyright 2013 by the Journal of Aerospace Information Systems.

The rectangles in Figure 5 on the far left denote the raw flight operational quality assurance (FOQA) data inputs from the aircraft. The data preparation module is where the domain expert typically identifies the types of data and selects, segregates, and normalizes the data variables. Because FAA criteria were used in the feature selection process, these functions as well as SME input, were not required. Additionally, in the feature construction module, the separated discrete and continuous data parameters undergo sequence construction and quantization. The goal of the detection module is to identify anomalous events of interest (outliers) at both the fleet and flight levels using the open-source multiple-kernel anomaly detection (MKAD) and index-Orca (iOrca) knowledge discovery algorithms, respectively. Then ranked data profiles are created from the processed datasets. During the knowledge discovery process in the post-processing module, the frequency and severity of the distance-based events are determined using the multivariate time series (MTS) tool and a sequence similarity search (S3). The anomalies are typically validated using domain field experts, text reports database (TRD), and flight crew interviews; however, FAA exceedance criteria precluded the necessity of a domain field expert, and TRD and flight crew narratives were not available. The last step of the knowledge discovery process is the generation of a report summarizing and visualizing the results.

Data and preprocessing. Raw FDM, or QAR data, from each aircraft, are collected for input into the AVSKD process. Each flight data record is constructed as a matrix with rows corresponding to time sampling, and columns to specific parameters. The sample rate can vary based on complexity of the QAR, with typical rates of 1 Hz and a flight record generating approximately 5000-6000 samples and up to approximately 300 parameters. Both discrete and continuous parameters are gathered. Data preparation is then conducted, with the raw data put through a data preparation module, which performs feature selection, data type segregation, missing data processing, noise filtering, and normalization.

Anomaly detection algorithms. Considering AVSKD is a flexible process, different types of ML algorithms can be integrated into the process. Thus, the algorithms selected and applied to the AVSKD process can vary based on the type of research being conducted. The six ML algorithms previously described were used to build predictive models based on cases determined to contain anomalous unstable approach events. Hui and Fanxing (2012) describe the difficulties encountered in data processing and introduce a symbolic aggregate approximation (SAX) algorithm to enhance the accuracy and performance of anomaly detection in QAR data. Even though the SAX algorithm experienced less than desirable accuracy, the research is indicative of the crucial role of algorithm in QAR flight data anomaly detection capability.

Knowledge discovery. Once anomalies have been discovered, the database is examined for frequency of events and for the purposes of predictive model building. Mathews et al. (2013) assert that validation of the events through domain expertise is typical and considered industry standard. Because FAA guidance was followed as the standard for feature selection, it was evident that the data variables used in the assessment of FAA exceedance criteria were valid. The final step in the AVSKD process is the reporting system. The reporting system consisted of figures representing important impact factors in the prediction of the target variable, UARM. The displays are percentage contributions for discrete variables, graphical plots for continuous variables, and percentage contributions of each continuous variable.

Sample, explore, modify, model, assess (SEMMA). The SAS Institute (Patel & Thompson, 2013) recommends using the SEMMA modeling process with SAS® Enterprise MinerTM. Specifically, the SEMMA acronym stands for Sample, Explore, Modify, Model, and Assess. The SEMMA process is iterative in nature, and the Sample or Explore stages were repeated after assessment of the model in order to make changes and then repeat the Model, Modify, and Assess processes (Maxson, 2018). This process was adapted for the study as illustrated in Figure 6.

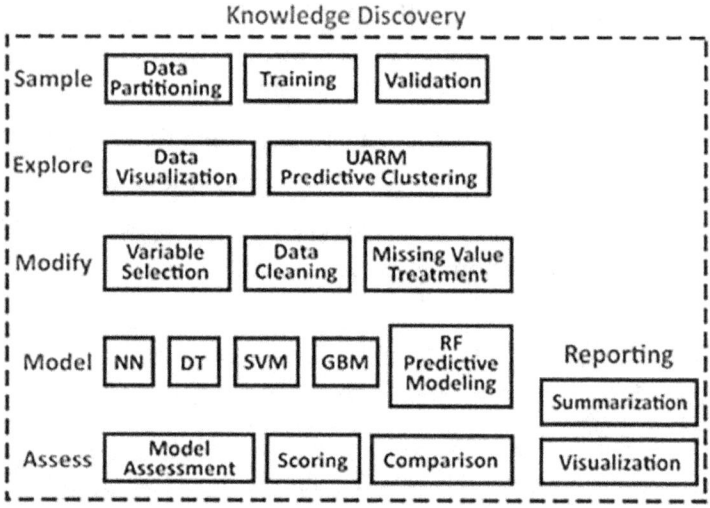

Figure 6. Sample, Explore, Modify, Model, Assess (SEMMA) knowledge discovery. UARM = Unstable Approach Risk Misperception; NN = neural network; DT = decision tree; SVM = support vector machine; GBM = gradient boost machine; RF = random forest. Adapted from "Prediction of Airport Arrival Rates Using Data Mining Methods" (Doctoral Dissertation) by R. W. Maxson, 2018, p. 70. Copyright 2018 by R. W. Maxson.

Sample. To begin the process, the data were inputted into the data mining software as input variables and a target variable is selected, e.g. UARM. The data were then partitioned into model training and validation subsets. The SAS© Enterprise Miner™ is compatible with many data input formats.

Explore. Once the data were uploaded into SAS Enterprise Miner™, the data were examined for missing variables, outliers, and/or skewed or peaked distributions. Several tools were available to use for these purposes; "StatExplore" was used for clustering, correlation, graphical investigation, and variable selection. The operational input and target variable were selected in the Sample module, and an iterative process included modifications after the data were inspected in the *Explore* step.

Modify. The purpose of this step was to prepare the data for model construction. This task could have been accomplished in several ways: inputting missing values, filtering the selected data, adding data to the set of data, merging the data with other sources, or partitioning the input data into smaller subsets. In this step, the data was further processed based on model construction requirements. Using the Model menu, "AutoNeural" was used to determine the most appropriate action for the NN, for example. Similarly, regarding regression model construction, data could have been transformed or imputed using dummy variables for categorical variables, and missing values could have either been removed or imputed (Maxson, 2018; Sarma, 2013).

Model. In this step, the prepared data were used to construct the models: decision trees, neural networks, regression, SVM, RFs, and GBMs. The software allowed flexibility in model construction depending on the data being used and the problem being investigated. Also, simultaneous model evaluations and comparisons were possible (Maxson, 2018; Sarma, 2013).

Assess. Finally, the models were compared and assessed using the model comparison function in the "Assess" menu grouping. Model assessment capability includes performance scores which are used to rank the models. ASE or misclassification rate could have been used to score the models and Receiver Operating Characteristic (ROC) and lift curves in the assessment of model performance (Maxson, 2018; Tufféry, 2011).

The purpose of this research was to utilize data mining techniques to explore a large-volume database of flight data recorder (FDR) data from commercial flight operations to predict *Unstable Approach Risk Misperception (UARM)*. The focus of this exploration was on the data generated beginning at the assessment window (500 ft AGL) to a point of either a landing or a rejected landing.

Variables were defined using the recorded flight data parameters, with FAA AC-120-71A providing guidance for variable selection for the *UARM* algorithm. For example, (a) target approach speed deviation, (b) flap position, (c) landing gear position, (d) engine speed, (e) altitude above ground level (AGL), and (f) glide path deviation are variables stated in the FAA stable approach criteria categories. Adherence to stable approach criteria was determined based on the data, including: (a) the vertical and lateral position of the aircraft with reference to the landing runway, (b) energy state, and (c) landing configuration. The information gathered in the data analysis was then used to predict the probability of the pilot misperceiving the runway excursion risk of continuing an unstable approach to landing.

Pilot misperception was represented by the decision to continue to a landing even when evidence exists of exceedance in any one or more of the flight data variables from the stabilized approach criteria, and for purposes of this research, was referred to as *UARM*. Data mining techniques were used to populate and compare various predictive models and to determine the most accurate model, which was then used to make predictions of the target variable.

The research was exploratory and data-driven in nature, based on the following research questions:

- How can the application of data-mining and machine learning techniques to recorded flight data be used to predict the probability of *Unstable Approach Risk Misperception* by the pilot?
- What flight data variables are the most important predictors of pilot misperception of a runway excursion hazard as evidenced by continuing an unstable approach to a landing?

The AVSKD data processing model was used to address data sampling, partitioning, and validation. This chapter describes in detail the step-by-step process that was used in the processing of the data and the predictive model construction. The SEMMA process was used to process the flight data sets integral to the SAS® EM™ predictive modeling software.

The research methodology chosen for the study was selected to build and test prediction models of UARM using large flight data. The research utilized predictive data mining methods, processes, and applications. Tufféry (2011) describes data mining as a method for exploring and analyzing large data with the purpose of discovering unknown or hidden patterns or relationships. In the research, data mining techniques were used to explore the approach and landing phases of flight for evidence of unstable approach criteria exceedance, as well as the presence, or not, of UARM. The flight data was explored to determine how unstable approaches and UARM could be measured. In order to answer the research questions, and to predict the probability that UARM would occur during an unstable approach, the following were used to build the models: (a) logistic regression, (b) decision tree, (c) neural network, (d) support vector machine, (e) gradient boost machine, and (f) random forest.

Flight-related variables representing approach speed, glide-slope deviation (i.e. vertical), localizer deviation (i.e. horizontal), aircraft landing configuration, engine thrust, vertical rate of descent, and altitude above ground level were anticipated to be the main focus of the models (see Table 3). Additionally, the occurrence of a rejected landing, or continued approach to landing, when confronted with evidence of an unstable approach, was also included. Flight variables for weight on wheels (WOW, > 0) and radar altimeter (RALT, > 0) were used to determine whether or not a rejected landing was executed.

Data mining was chosen to be the appropriate method for the research based on the goal of exploring very large flight data. The AVSKD data processing model was used as a framework for the exploration of large data collected by the flight data recorders on aircraft operating in the NAS. The data sets used for this research were assembled by NASA and are publicly available. Mathews et al (2013) have validated the AVSKD process.

As previously described, sampling of the data included only the portion of the flight from 500 feet above ground level, during the approach phase, to a point when either a landing, or a rejected landing, was evident. Although 186 variables were available in the FDM data, those variables affecting one of three areas (energy state, aircraft configuration, and aircraft relative position to the landing runway) were initially examined in the feature selection process.

The sampled data was restricted to the approach and landing phase of flight, beginning at 500 AGL until either a landing or a rejected landing was performed. Figure 7 shows the points at which data was collected.

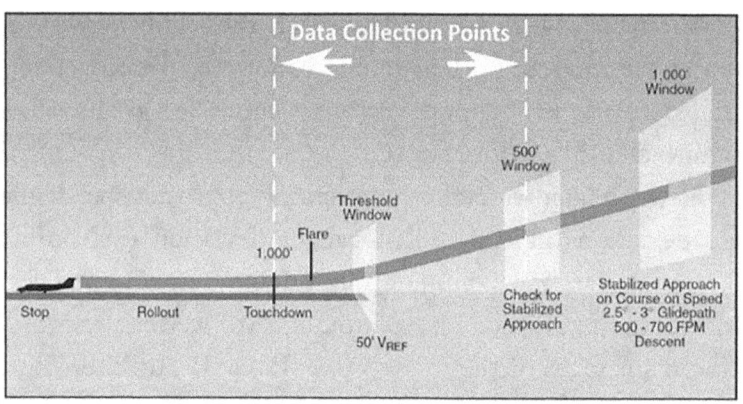

Figure 7. Data collection points. Adapted from "Air Traffic Bulletin Procedures (ATB 2019-1)," by Federal Aviation Administration Air Traffic Procedures, April 2019, p. 2. Retrieved from https://www.faa.gov/air_traffic/publications/media/atb_april_2019.pdf

Data Coding and Algorithm Development

Flight-related variables representing: (a) approach speed, (b) glideslope deviation (i.e. vertical), (c) localizer deviation (i.e.

horizontal), (d) aircraft landing configuration, (e) engine thrust, (f) vertical rate of descent, and (g) altitude above ground level were anticipated to be the main focus of the models.

The archived data have been collected for each flight in matrix format with each row corresponding to snapshot in time, and each column corresponding to each flight variable. The acquisition of these data represented an opportunity for aviation research, with the application of data mining techniques as a strategy to discover empirical relationships between the variables captured in large data. The data was explored to determine instances when FAA stable approach criteria were not met, and then whether a landing or rejected landing was executed. As presented in Figure 8, only the approach to a landing, or rejected landing, was examined in the exploration of the data.

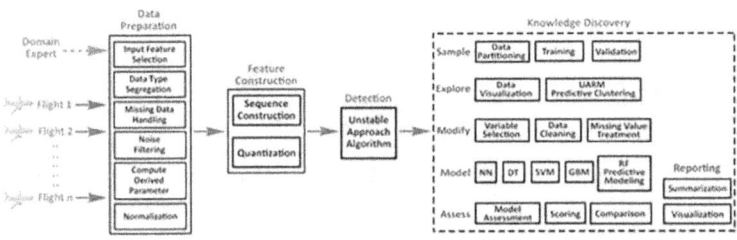

Figure 8. Research procedure framework. UARM = Unstable Approach Risk Misperception; NN = neural network; DT = decision tree; SVM = support vector machine; GBM = gradient boost machine; RF = random forest. Adapted from "Discovering Anomalous Aviation Safety Events Using Scalable Data Mining Algorithms," by B. Matthews, S. Das, K. Bhaduri, K. Das, R. Martin, and N. Oza, 2013, Journal of Aerospace Information Systems, 10(10), p. 469. Copyright 2013 by the Journal of Aerospace Information System, and from "Prediction of Airport Arrival Rates Using Data Mining Methods" (Doctoral Dissertation) by R. W. Maxson, 2018, p. 70. Copyright 2018 by R. W. Maxson.

Both flow chart and pseudo code was used to represent the algorithm in the research. Kommadi (2019) describes how keywords, documentation, and action tasks can assist in the visualization of the algorithm. The researcher continues to compare and contrast flow chart representations of algorithms. Algorithms depict the process of problem solving, decision making, and logic applications. Flow charts use symbols in series to provide a visual representation of the problem to be considered and the AVSKD data process was applied to FDR data. The process followed analysis based on consideration of approach/unstable approach evidence, and the decision to either continue to landing or to execute a rejected landing. The flow chart representing this logic process is presented in **Figure 9**.

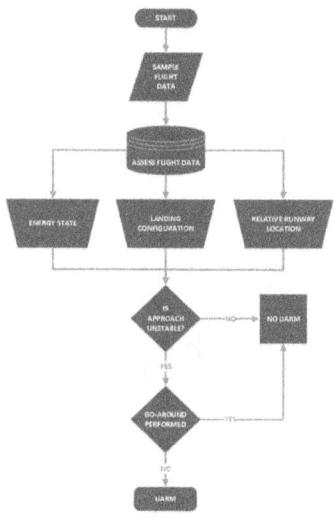

Figure 9. Unstable Approach Risk Misperception Algorithm Flow Diagram.

Once evidence of unstable approaches was discovered using a simple algorithm-based anomaly detection technique, the frequency and result (presence or not of UARM) was then determined

As described in the literature review, Sarma (2013) presents an outline of the data analysis approach. The data process at this point in the AVSKD process then entered the feature selection mode. The algorithm constructed for the "detection" phase of the process was also applied to allow for the process to continue to the "detection" phase, where the models were trained and validated, as depicted in Figure 5. These procedures, as well as those detailed by the SAS Institute, which recommends using a SEMMA modeling process, comprised the methods used for building the predictive models. SEMMA includes *Sample, Explore, Modify, Model,* and *Assess*. The SAS® Enterprise Miner™ software package was utilized for this purpose based on the data mining methodology described. The SEMMA process is iterative in nature and the repetition of variable selection was conducted based on gained familiarity and relationships among variables as they were discovered. Thus, the *Model, Modify,* and *Assess* processes was repeated as modeling strategies evolved.

The FDR and all data contained therein were de-identified by NASA prior to release for research, hence the archived data measurement device is considered to be a valid and reliable representation of FAA certified FDR equipment. These measurement and collection devices provide real time flight data and are measured and collected by FDR and CVR devices, as well as the more recently developed Quick Access Recorder (QAR). Walker (2017) asserts that the QAR has developed into a superior data collection device and is now considered industry standard. This development of the QAR has enabled data to be conveniently extracted from commercial transport aircraft with recent systems integrated into wireless systems (Walker, 2017).

A target variable, UARM, representing the occurrence of pilots continuing an unstable approach to landing was identified and treated as a binary variable. For example, when the aircraft is on approach at 500 feet AGL, an assessment window for the pilot to examine specific flight parameters and assess aircraft performance based on the FAA stable approach criteria opens. As part of the landing checklist, the pilot monitoring (PM) observes and calls out deviations (if any) on descent rate, approach speed, glide path position, localizer, and landing configuration (e.g. landing gear down, flaps in landing position, and speed brakes stowed).

In the event that uncorrected deviations exist and exceed FAA criteria, a rejected landing maneuver is recommended by the FAA and standard operating procedures (IATA, 2017).

NASA has provided public access to FDR data, which was gathered from 35 regional jets operating in the NAS. Data mining techniques were utilized to address the nature of the research. Specifically, the AVSKD process provided the framework for the treatment of the data as well as the discovery of unstable approaches and evidence of the occurrence or the absence of UARM. The SEMMA process was then be applied to the data, with the construction and evaluation of predictive models. These NASA FDR data were modeled using: (a) decision trees, (b) neural networks, (c) logistic regression, (d) SVM, (e) RF, and (f) GBM predictive models. Model performance was compared and tested, with the goal of predicting the probability of UARM in the event an unstable approach occurs

Data Analysis Results

FDR data were achieved and made available by NASA for public use. These FDR data were collected from a fleet of 35 regional jets operating in the National Airspace System. The research was based on the ability to use FDR data to train and validate the machine learning-based models. The data was partitioned and a separate portion of the data was used to score the 3 branch DT model. The data was used to construct (a) decision tree with 2, 3 and 5 branches, (b) logistic regression, (c) neural network, (d) support vector machine, (e) gradient boost machine, and (f) random forest models. A model comparison was used to determine that the 3 branch Decision Tree model had the highest predictive power, with a 98.8% prediction score. Once DT was determined to be the highest scoring model, it was used to (a) determine the predictive probability of the target variable, UARM, and (b) rank input variables in order of importance.

The combined data sets were partitioned 50/50 percent to train, validate, and compare the performance of all of the models. The data was then used to score the DT (3 branches) model by using the Score node within the SAS® EM™. The scored data resulted in predictive probabilities of UARM that were then compared with the actual UARM instances that were observed. These results are included in subsequent sections of this chapter.

Mathews et al. (2013) asserted that once anomalous events are detected using the knowledge discovery algorithm, validation is generally performed in three ways: (a) domain expert input, (b) ASRS pilot narrative reports, and/or (c) pilot interviews. As the AVSKD process was validated in previous research, domain expertise was represented by using FAA guidelines as the basis of feature selection. One advantage of using FAA unstable approach criteria was that any potential bias was eliminated regarding feature selection.

As part of the model training and validation process, various combinations of input variables were selected for testing. The first variable input combinations used all of the flight data variables available in each of the data sets used. Variables in the data set used to describe aircraft specific FMS software version updates, as well as date and time data, were rejected in early iterations. The iterative process dictated that subsequent model construction was based on feature selection using estimates of variable importance. For example, initial runs resulted in MNS (selected Mach speed) included in the predictive modeling process. Selected Mach was determined to be a variable associated with the cruise (enroute) flight phase, and was not determined to be associated with, or relevant to, the approach and landing phases of flight (a delimitation in the study used to develop the UARM algorithm). Therefore, MNS was rejected in further iterations of the model runs. Ultimately a predictive power score of 98.8% was achieved with the highest scoring model, 3 branch DT. Additionally, variable importance regarding the occurrence of UARM was determined and is reported in tables listed in subsequent sections of this section.

One of the most important objectives of the study was to develop an algorithm for the target variable, UARM. In order to successfully accomplish this task, it was first necessary to identify unstable approaches within the data. Initial examination of the data indicated the recorded flight data contained variables that could be used to represent FAA exceedance criteria for unstable approaches. Results of this determination also indicated that flight data variables could be used to develop the algorithm for UARM.

Once this determination was made, a coding process was developed to create a data variable representing landing, rejected landing, and UARM. One important step in this process was the development of assessment criteria limitations as presented in subsequent sections. For example, weight on wheels (WOW>0) was used to determine if a landing (or rejected landing, WOW=0) was accomplished. Exceedance of any of the flight variables used in the construction of stable approach criteria (energy state, landing configuration, location relative runway) was successfully used to determine if an unstable approach was evident. These variables used to identify unstable approaches were selected based on the measurement of these three constructs used by the FAA to define and describe an unstable approach.

A straightforward *If/Then* decision process was then developed and used to complete the UARM algorithm (See Figure 8). Results of this If/Then assessment process were successful in the discovery that evidence of UARM had occurred or not. For example, once an unstable approach was identified, a determination was made whether or not a rejected landing was performed. *If* evidence of an unstable approach was indicated, and a rejected landing was not performed, *then* UARM resulted. Results of this UARM algorithm development were then successfully used to construct predictive models as well as the identification of UARM.

The rest of the flight data variables, including those representing the FAA stable approach criteria, were utilized as input variables and were anticipated to be continuous or categorical. For example, approach speed was expected be continuous, based on numerical values while landing gear position was expected to be categorical (i.e. either up or down). Sarma (2013) described the process of *binning* to classify continuous variables in a categorical manner.

An important aspect of the UARM algorithm development was that of feature selection. The iterative process was used to reject or accept flight data variables based on decision making rules established and described in the UARM algorithm. In order to preclude selection bias, FAA stable approach criteria were used to identify flight data variables which represented stable approach assessment. Results indicated that the *Explore* node was quite useful in the iterative process of feature selection. For example, because unstable approach was a prerequisite for UARM, it was obviously a predictor of the occurrence of UARM. Accordingly, failure to reject the landing during an unstable approach was also a prerequisite for UARM and was therefore anticipated to be present in 100% of UARM occurrences.

One key element in the development of the UARM algorithm was the ability to make the important distinction between the identification and analysis of unstable approaches and the ability to successfully predict the probability of occurrence of UARM. For example, exceedance of approach speed criteria at the assessment point would be an indication of an unstable approach, but not necessarily an indication of the probability of the occurrence of UARM if the pilot rejected the landing.

Results indicated that one advantage of the UARM algorithm was that of scalability. Several different predictive models successfully utilized the UARM algorithm with the application of recorded flight data. Results demonstrated that real world recorded flight data was successfully assessed in the UARM algorithm process to predict the probability of occurrence of the target variable. The UARM algorithm was successfully used repeatedly with consistent results to evaluate large recorded flight data. The algorithm was successfully developed based on initial data coding, subsequent use of an If/Then decision-making process, and ultimately the extremely accurate and precise predictive power regarding the target variable, UARM. The UARM algorithm provided a step by step, repeatable process to the analysis of recorded flight data and allowed for a reliable and valid methodology for the analysis of FDR data to predict UARM. Evidence of successful employment of the UARM algorithm is presented in subsequent sections. The recorded flight data was then examined for evidence of unstable approaches. Using FAA exceedance criteria as previously described, unstable approaches were extracted and examined for causal factors (i.e., exceedance of FAA flight parameters). Flight data variables associated with FAA unstable approach exceedance variables were also examined to determine frequency data. Frequency data for approaches and occurrence of UARM is presented in Table 1. Although assumptions of normality and multicollinearity were not required to be met for the machine learning algorithms utilized in predictive model building, the exceedance criteria variables were examined for general consistency and to better visualize the data. Results of the descriptive analysis are presented in Table 2. Fight data variable exceedances are summarized in Table 3. Exceedance criteria for glideslope deviation was observed most frequently, landing configuration deviations second (power levers at idle, engine thrust not stable) with localizer deviation (lateral distance from extended runway centerline) third most frequent.

Pressing On

Table 1 Summary of Recorded Flight Data Approach Frequencies

Approach Classification	N	Percentage
Total Approaches	152,442	
Unstable	11,348	7.44
Stable	141,094	92.6
Rejected Landings	450	0.29
Landings	151,992	99.7
UARM	11,047	7.24

Source: Adapted from "Sample flight data for 35 aircraft," by National Aeronautics and Space Administration DASHlink, 2012. Retrieved from https://c3.nasa.gov/DASHlink/projects/85/resources/?type=ds. *Note. UARM=Unstable Approach Risk Misperception.*

Table 2 Summary of Unstable Approach Criteria Descriptive Statistics

Variable	N	Missing	M	Min	Max	Skewness	Kurtosis
IVV	33	0	-659(109)	029	1675	0.280	17.4
GS	349	0	119(12.1)	104	179	6.452	180.0
ALTR	34	0	-670(204)	005	1685	0.097	10.5
CAS	156	0	124(7.61)	104	179	1.25	159.0
LGDN	359	0					
PLA	3124	0					
Flap	64	0					
DA	383	0	0.34(0.041)	0.02	5.5	-0.517	27.2
LOC	2742	0	0.071(0.020)	0.001	1.7	-2.02	52.4
GLS	4338	0	0.082(0.003)	0.001	2.6	-1.83	30.4

Note. LGDN, PLA, and FLAP are categorical variables, and are presented for informational purposes in order to include the complete list of unstable approach criteria variables. IVV = Inertial Vertical Velocity. FPM = Feet Per Minute. GS = Ground Speed. ALTR = Altitude Rate. CAS = Calibrated Airspeed. LGDN = Landing Gear Down. PLA = Power Lever Angle. DA = Drift Angle. LOC = Localizer. GLS = Glideslope. SD = Standard Deviation.

Table 3 Summary of Unstable Approach Flight Data Variable Exceedance Frequency

Unstable approach Construct	Flight Data Variables	Exceedance Frequency
Energy State	IVV	33
	GS	349
	ALTR	34
	CAS	456
Landing Configuration	LGDN	359
	PLA	3124
	FLAP	1159
Relative Runway Location	DA	383
	LOC	2742
	GLS	4338

Source: Adapted from "Sample flight data for 35 aircraft," by National Aeronautics and Space Administration DASHlink, 2012. Retrieved from https://c3.nasa.gov/DASHlink/projects/85/resources/?type=ds. Note. IVV = Inertial Vertical Velocity. FPM = Feet Per Minute. GS = Ground Speed. ALTR = Altitude Rate. CAS = Calibrated Airspeed. LGDN = Landing Gear Down. PLA = Power Lever Angle. DA = Drift Angle. LOC = Localizer. GLS = Glideslope.

NASA has provided public access to FDR data, which was gathered from 35 regional jets operating in the NAS. Data mining techniques were utilized to address the nature of the research. Specifically, the successful development and deployment of the UARM algorithm and the procedural guidelines of AVSKD process provided the framework for the treatment of the data as well as the discovery of unstable approaches and evidence of the occurrence or the absence of UARM. The SEMMA process was then successfully applied to the data, with the construction and evaluation of predictive models. These NASA FDR data were modeled using: (a) decision trees with 2, 3, and 5 branches, (b) neural networks, (c) logistic regression, (d) support vector machine, (e) random forest and, (f) gradient boost machine predictive models.

Model performance was compared and tested, and achieved the goal of predicting the probability of UARM in the event an unstable approach occurs at 98%. Once the models were analyzed, a successful determination of how DM techniques could be utilized to predict UARM, and which were the most important predictors to the probability of UARM, was determined.

DEFINITIONS

AVSKD Aviation Safety Knowledge Discovery Process. The process of analyzing aviation data, beginning with the collection of raw FOQA or FDM data via aircraft flight data recorders, though several phases: data preparation, detection, feature selection, and knowledge discovery. For the purposes of the research study, the AVSKD process concludes with the assessment of predictive models, as described in Chapter III (Mathews et al., 2013).

Data Mining Data mining is the set of methods and techniques for exploring and analyzing large data sets, in order to find certain unknown or hidden rules, associations or tendencies. It is the art of extracting information (knowledge) from the data. For the purposes of the study, predictive data mining techniques are used to extrapolate new information based on the present information (Tufféry, 2011, p. 4).

Decision Tree A decision tree represents a hierarchical segmentation of the data and is composed of a set of rules that can be applied to partition the data into disjoint groups (Sarma, 2013, p. 196).

Energy State Management The interrelationship between kinetic energy (airspeed), potential energy (altitude), and chemical energy (power). Refers to pilot energy state management technique options available for pilots to change or maintain a safe and stable energy state, including external factors and corrective techniques (FAA, 2017a, p. 3).

Gradient Boost Machine A form of ML technique, using ensemble learning, used in the construction of predictive models, generally classification and regression. Typically, weaker decision trees are used in the ensemble.

Neural Networks A neural network is a complex nonlinear function of inputs, divided into different layers and different units within each layer. A large number of nonlinear functions can be generated and fitted to the data by means of different architectural specifications (Sarma, 2013, p. 362). This architecture can be based on that of the brain, organized in neurons and synapses, and takes the form of interconnected units (or formal neurons), with each continuous input variable corresponding to a unit at a first level, called the input layer, and each category of a qualitative variable also corresponding to a unit of the input layer (Tufféry, 2011, p. 217).

Random Forest A form of ML learning, using ensemble learning for purposes of classification and regression. Builds models consisting of multiple decision trees for training and produces a mode of classes or mean prediction of the individual decision tree models.

Runway Excursion This term is limited to veer off or overrun from the runway surface that occurs while an aircraft is landing, based mainly on an unstable approach (FAA, 2014).

SAS® Enterprise Miner™ SAS® Enterprise Miner™ is a software package consisting of different levels of data, such as textual or numeric, and was used for the construction and analysis of predictive models. SAS EM utilizes machine-learning algorithms that streamline the data mining process and create highly accurate predictive and descriptive models that are based on analysis of vast amounts of data (Sarma, 2013).

Stabilized Approach Concept "A stabilized approach is characterized by a constant-angle, constant-rate of descent approach profile ending near the touchdown point, where the landing maneuver begins" (FAA, 2003, Appendix 2, para 2). The energy state, landing configuration, aircraft location approach criteria are applied at 500 ft height above touchdown.

Standard Operating Procedures Aircrew procedures developed by an airline for normal, abnormal, and emergency procedure compliance to ensure safe, efficient, and on-time flight performance (Giles, 2013).

Support Vector Machine A machine learning model using algorithms that analyze data for classification and regression analysis. SVMs can perform both linear and non-linear classification using the *kernel trick*. SVMs can be used in both supervised and non-supervised approaches, in addition to clustering techniques in data analysis (Lauer & Bloch, 2008).

Unstable Approach Risk Misperception Pilot lapses in aeronautical decision making occurring when evidence of an unstable approach exists, and the pilot elects to continue the approach to a landing, risking a runway excursion (FAA, 2014).

ACRONYMS

AC	Advisory Circular
ADM	Aeronautical Decision Making
ADM	Aircraft Diagnostic and Maintenance System
ADS-B	Automatic Dependent Surveillance-Broadcast
AGL	Above Ground Level
AOM	Aircraft Operating Manual
ASPM	Aviation System Performance Metrics
ASRS	Aviation Safety Reporting System
AVSKD	Aviation Safety Knowledge Discovery Process
BADA	Base of Aircraft Data
BCA	Boeing Commercial Airplanes
BLS	Bureau of Labor Statistics
CART	Classification and Regression Tree
CAST	Commercial Aviation Safety Team
CEDAR	Comprehensive Electronic Data Analysis and Reporting
CFR	Code of Federal Regulations
CI	Cost Index
CRM	Crew Resource Management
CVR	Cockpit Voice Recorder
DH	Decision Height
DWH	Data Warehouse
EFIS	Electronic Flight Instrument System
FAA	Federal Aviation Administration
FDM	Flight Data Monitoring
FDR	Flight Data Recorder
FOQA	Flight Operations Quality Assurance
FSF	Flight Safety Foundation
GA	General Aviation
HAS	Hazardous Attitude Scale
HBAT	Handbook Bulletin for Air Transportation
HIP	Human Information Processing
IATA	International Air Transport Association
ICAO	International Civil Aviation Organization
IFR	Instrument Flight Rules

ILS	Instrument Landing System
IMC	Instrument Meteorological Conditions
LOSA	Line Operations Safety Audit
MKAD	Multiple kernel anomaly detection
ML	Machine Learning
MLM	Multilevel Modeling
MTS	Multi-variate Time Series Search
NAS	National Airspace System
NASA	National Aeronautics and Space Administration
ND	Navigational Display
NOAA	National Oceanic Atmospheric Administration
NTSB	National Transportation Safety Board
OPSPECS	Operations Specifications
PFD	Primary Flight Display
POI	Principal Operations Inspector
RE	Runway Excursion
SA	Situation Awareness
SMS	Safety Management Systems
SOP	Standard Operating Procedures
SVM	Support Vector Machine
TAWS	Terrain Awareness and Warning System
TEM	Threat Error Management
TOD	Top of Descent
UARM	Unstable Approach Risk Misperception
UPS	United Parcel Service
VFR	Visual Flight Rules
VIPR	Vehicle Integrated Prognostics Reasoner
VMC	Visual Meteorological Conditions
WOW	Weight on Wheels

REFERENCES

Achenbach, A., & Spinler, S. (2018). Prescriptive analytics in airline operations: Arrival time prediction and cost index optimization for short-haul flights. *Operations Research Perspectives, 5*, 265-279. doi:10.1016/j.orp.2018.08.004

Alligier, R., & Gianazza, D. (2018). Learning aircraft operational factors to improve aircraft climb prediction: A large scale multi-airport study. *Transportation Research Part C, 96*, 72-95. doi:10.1016/j.trc.2018.08.012

Aircraft Accident Investigation Board Pakistan [AAIBP]. (2020). *Accident of flight PK8303 Airbus A320-214 AP-BLD crashed near Karachi airport on 22-05-2020.* (Preliminary Investigation Report). Karachi, Pakistan: Author. Retrieved from https://www.caapakistan.com.pk/Upload/SIBReports/AAIB-431.pdf

Aslaner, H. E., Unal, C., & Iyigun, C. (2016). Applying data mining techniques to detect abnormal flight characteristics. *Proceedings of the SPIE, Vol. 9850* (pp. 1-19). doi:10.1117/12.2224061

Benbassat, D., & Abramson, C. I. (2002). Landing flare accident reports and pilot perception analysis. *The International Journal of Aviation Psychology, 12*(2), 137-152. doi:10.1207/S15327108IJAP1202_3

Biswas, G., Mack, D., Mylaraswamy, D., & Bharadwaj, R. (2013). *Data mining for anomaly detection.* Hampton: NASA/Langley Research Center. Retrieved from Advanced Technologies & Aerospace Collection; ProQuest Central (20130011182).

Blair, B., Lee, H. K. H., & Davies, M. (2017). Real-time detection of in-flight aircraft damage. *Journal of Classification, 34*(3), 494-513. https://doi.org/10.1007/s0035

Boeing Commercial Airlines, Aviation Safety. (2017). *Statistical summary of commercial jet airplane accidents worldwide operations 1959 – 2016.* Seattle, WA: Author. Retrieved from https://www.skybrary.aero/bookshelf/books/4239.pdf

Breiman, L. (1997). *Arcing the edge* (Technical Report 486). Department of Statistics, University of California, Berkeley. Retrieved from https://statistics.berkeley.edu/tech-reports/486

Breiman, L. (2001). Random forests. *Machine Learning. 45(*1), pp. 5-32. doi:10.1023/A:101933404324

Brueckner, J. K., & Pai, V. (2009). Technological innovation in the airline industry: The impact of regional jets. *International Journal of Industrial Organization, 27*(1), 110-120. doi:10.1016/j.ijindorg.2008.05.003

Budalakoti, S., Budalakoti, S., Srivastava, A. N., & Otey, M. E. (2009). Anomaly detection and diagnosis algorithms for discrete symbol sequences with applications to airline safety. *IEEE Transactions on Systems, Man, and Cybernetics, Part C (Applications and Reviews), 39*(1), 101-113. doi:10.1109/TSMCC.2008.2007248

Campbell, A., Zaal, P., Schroeder, J. & Shah, S. (2018). *Development of possible go-around criteria for transport aircraft.* Paper presented at 2018 Aviation Technology, Integration, and Operations Conference. doi:10.2514/6.2018-3198

Chang, Y., Yang, H., & Hsiao, Y. (2016). Human risk factors associated with pilots in runway excursions. *Accident Analysis and Prevention, 94*, 227-237. doi:10.1016/j.aap.2016.06.007

Chen, J., Zhang, X., Zhao, M., & Xia, Y. (2017). Research on extraction of QAR key parameters during approach phase of civil aviation. *Advances in Materials, Machinery, Electrical Engineering (AMMEE 2017).* Atlantis Press.

Chidambaram, S., & Srinivasagan, K. G. (2018). Performance evaluation of support vector machine classification approaches in data mining. *Cluster Computing.* Springer. doi:10.1007/s10586-018-2036-z

Christopher, A. B. A., Vivekanandam, V. S., Anderson, A. B. A., Markkandeyan, S., & Sivakumar, V. (2016). Large-scale data analysis on aviation accident database using different data mining techniques. *The Aeronautical Journal, 120*(1234), 1849–1866. doi:10.1017/aer.2016.107

Curtis, T., Rhoades, D. L., & Waguespack, B. P., Jr. (2013). *Regional jet aircraft competitiveness: Challenges and opportunities.* Retrieved from https://commons.erau.edu/cgi/viewcontent.cgi?article=1076&context=publication

Das, S., Matthews, B. L., & Lawrence, R. (2011). Fleet level anomaly detection of aviation safety data. *IEEE Conference on Prognostics and Health Management* (pp. 1-10). doi:10.1109/ICPHM.2011.6024356

Das, S., Li, L., Srivastava, A., & Hansman, R. J. (2010). Comparison of algorithms for anomaly detection in flight recorder data of airline operations. *12th AIAA Aviation Technology, Integration, and Operations (ATIO) Conference* (pp. 1-26). doi:10.2514/6.2012-5593

Diallo, O. (2012). A predictive aircraft landing speed model using neural network. *IEEE 31st Digital Avionics Systems Conference* (pp. 1-33). doi:10.1109/DASC.2012.638215

Dismukes, R. K. (2010). Understanding and analyzing human error in real-world operations. In *Human factors in aviation* (pp. 335-374). Academic Press.

Dubey, A., Kamath, S., & Kanakia, D. (2016). Learning data mining techniques. *International Journal of Computer Applications 136*(11), 5-8.

DVB Bank SE. (2019). *An overview of commercial aircraft 2018-2019*. Retrieved from https://www.dvbbank.com/~/media/Files/D/dvb-bank-corp/aviation/dvb-overview-of-commercial-aircraft-2018-2019.pdf

Federal Aviation Administration. [FAA]. (1991). *Aeronautical decision making* (Advisory Circular 60-22). https://www.faa.gov/documentLibrary/media/Advisory_Circular/AC_60-22.pdf

Federal Aviation Administration. [FAA]. (2003). *Standard operating procedures for flight deck crewmembers* (Advisory Circular 120-71A [Cancelled]). https://www.faa.gov/documentLibrary/media/Advisory_Circular/AC120-71A.pdf

Federal Aviation Administration. [FAA]. (2004). *Flight operational quality assurance* (Advisory Circular 120-82). https://www.faa.gov/documentLibrary/media/Advisory_Circular/AC_120-82.pdf

Federal Aviation Administration. [FAA]. (2005). *Runway length requirements for airport design* (Advisory Circular 150/5325-4B). https://www.faa.gov/documentLibrary/media/advisory_circular/150-5325-4B/150_5325_4b.pdf

Federal Aviation Administration. [FAA]. (2007a). *Introduction to safety management systems (SMS) for airport operators*. Advisory Circular 150/5200-37. Washington, DC: Author.

Federal Aviation Administration. [FAA]. (2007b). *Flight standards information management system (FSIMS)* (Order 8900.1). Washington, DC: Author. Retrieved from https://www.faa.gov/documentLibrary/media/Order/8900.1.pdf

Federal Aviation Administration. [FAA]. (2011). *Continuous descent final approach*. Advisory Circular 120-108. Washington, DC: Author.

Federal Aviation Administration. [FAA]. (2012). *Aircraft approach category*. Safety Alert for Operators: SAFO 12005. Washington, DC: Author.

Federal Aviation Administration. [FAA]. (2013). *Operational use of flight path management systems*. Final Report of the Performance-Based operations Aviation Rulemaking Committee/Commercial Aviation Safety Team Flight Deck Automation Working Group. Washington, DC: Author. Retrieved from https://www.faa.gov/aircraft/air_cert/design_approvals/human_factors/media/oufpms_report.pdf

Federal Aviation Administration. [FAA]. (2014a). *Mitigating the risks of a runway overrun upon landing*. Advisory Circular 91-79A. Washington, DC: Author.

Federal Aviation Administration. [FAA]. (2014b). *FAA approval of aviation training devices and their use for training and experience*. Advisory Circular 61-136A. Washington, DC: Author.

Federal Aviation Administration. [FAA]. (2015). *National runway safety report*. Washington, DC: Author. Retrieved from https://www.faa.gov/airports/runway_safety/publications/media/Runway-Safety-Report-2013-14.pdf

Federal Aviation Administration. [FAA]. (2016). *Pilot's handbook of aeronautical knowledge* (FAA-H-8083-25). Washington, DC: Author. Retrieved from https://www.faa.gov/regulations_policies/handbooks_manuals/aviation/phak/media/pilot_handbook.pdf

Federal Aviation Administration. [FAA]. (2017a). *Upset prevention and recovery training*. Advisory Circular 120-111. Washington, DC: Author.

Federal Aviation Administration. [FAA]. (2017b). *FAA aerospace forecast, fiscal years 2017-2037*. Washington, DC; Author. Retrieved from https://www.faa.gov/data_research/aviation/aerospace_forecasts/media/fy2017-37_faa_aerospace_forecast.pdf

Federal Aviation Administration. [FAA]. (2018). *FAA stabilized approach and go-around concept*. FAA Safety Brief 18-09. (FAA-AFS-920-18-09). Washington, DC: Author. Retrieved from https://www.faa.gov/news/safety_briefing/2018/media/SE_Topic_18-09.pdf

Federal Aviation Administration. [FAA]. (2019). *Air traffic procedures air traffic bulletin procedures* (ATB 2019-1). Washington, DC: Author. Retrieved from https://www.faa.gov/air_traffic/publications/media/atb_april_2019.pdf

Flight Safety Foundation. [FSF]. (2009). FSF ALAR Briefing Note 7.1: Stabilized approach. *Flight Safety Foundation Approach and Landing Accident Reduction tool kit*. Flight Safety Foundation: Alexandria, VA. Retrieved from https://www.skybrary.aero/bookshelf/books/864.pdf

Forlizzi, L., Güting, R. H., Nardelli, E., & Schneider, M. (2000). *A data model and data structures for moving objects databases, 29*(2), 319-330. ACM.

Friedman, J. H. (2001). Greedy function approximation: A gradient boosting machine. *The Annals of Statistics, 29*(5), 1189-1232. doi:10.1214/aos/1013203451

Friso, H. F., Richard, C., Visser, H. G., Vincent, T., & Bruno, D. (2018). Predicting abnormal runway occupancy times and observing related precursors. *Journal of Aerospace Information Systems, 15*(1), 10-21. doi:10.2514/1.I010548

Gallego, C. E., Gómez Comendador, V. F., Sáez Nieto, F. J., Orenga Imaz, G., & Arnaldo Valdés, R. M. (2018). Analysis of air traffic control operational impact on aircraft vertical profiles supported by machine learning. *Transportation Research Part C, (95)*, 883-903. doi:10.1016/j.trc.2018.03.017

Genuer, R., Poggi, J., Tuleau-Malot, C., & Villa-Vialaneix, N. (2017). Random forests for big data. *Big Data Research, 9*, 28-46. doi:10.1016/j.bdr.2017.07.003

Gera, M., & Goel, S. (2015). Data mining-techniques, methods and algorithms: A review on tools and their validity. *International Journal of Computer Algorithms 113*(18), 22-29.

Ghoson, A. M. A. (2011). Decision tree induction & clustering techniques in SAS Enterprise Miner, SPSS Clemintine, and IBM intelligent miner-a comparative analysis. *International Journal of Management & Information Systems 14*(3)*)*, 57-70. doi:10.19030/ijmis.v14i3.841

Giles, C. N. (2013). Modern airline pilots' quandary: Standard operating procedures--to comply or not to comply. *Journal of Aviation Technology and Engineering, 2*(2), 1. doi:10.7771/2159-6670.1070

Gorinevsky, D., Mathews, B., & Martin, R. (2012). Aircraft anomaly detection using performance models trained on fleet data. *2012 Conference on Intelligent Data Understanding* (pp. 17-23). doi:10.1109/CIDU.2012.6382

Gregorutti, B., Michel, B., & Saint-Pierre, P. (2015; 2014). Grouped variable importance with random forests and application to multiple functional data analysis. *Computational Statistics and Data Analysis, 90*, 15-35. doi:10.1016/j.csda.2015.04.002

Hapfelmeier, A., & Ulm, K. (2014). Variable selection by random forests using data with missing values. *Computational Statistics and Data Analysis, 80*, 129-139. doi:10.1016/j.csda.2014.06.017

Hu, C., Zhou, S., Xie, Y., & Chang, W. (2016). The study on hard landing prediction model with optimized parameter SVM method. *Proceedings of the 35th Chinese Control Conference* (pp. 4283-4287). doi:10.1109/ChiCC.2016.7554018

Hui, Y., & Fanxing, M. (2012). Application of improved SAX algorithm to QAR flight data. *Physics Procedia (24)* 1406-1413. 2012 International Conference on Applied Physics and Industrial Engineering.

Hunter, D. R. (2005). Measurement of hazardous attitudes among pilots. *The International Journal of Aviation Psychology, 15*(1), 23-43. doi:10.1207/s15327108ijap1501_2

International Air Transport Association [IATA] (2017). *Unstable approach: Risk mitigation, policies, procedures and best practices, 3rd edition.* Montreal: Author. Retrieved from https://www.canso.org/system/files/Unstable%20Approaches%203rd%20Edition.pdf

Ju, C., Ji, M., Lan, J., & You, X. (2017). Narcissistic personality and risk perception among Chinese aviators: The mediating role of promotion focus. *International Journal of Psychology, 52*(S1), 1-8. doi:10.1002/ijop.12243

Ju, X. & Tian, Y. (2012). Knowledge-based support vector machine classifiers via nearest points. *Procedia Computer Science, (9)*, 1240-1248.

Kang, L., & Hansen, M. (2018). Improving airline fuel efficiency via fuel burn prediction and uncertainty estimation. *Transportation Research Part C, 97*, 128-146. doi:10.1016/j.trc.2018.10.002

Koteeswaran, S., Malarvizhi, N., Kannan, E., Sasikala, S., & Geetha, S. (2017). Data mining application on aviation accident data for predicting topmost causes for accidents. *Cluster Computing*. doi:10.1007/s10586-017-1394-2

Kumar, A., & Ghosh, A. K. (2019). Decision tree and random forest–based novel unsteady aerodynamics modeling using flight data. *Journal of Aircraft, 56*(1), 403-409. doi:10.2514/1.C035034

Kumar, V., Pang-Ning, T, & Steinbach, M. (2018). Data mining. In D. Mehta & S Sahni (Eds.), *Handbook of data structures and applications (2nd ed.)*, *(pp. 997-1012)*. Portland: CRC Press

Kommadi, B. (2019). *Learn data structures and algorithms with golang*. Birmingham, UK: Packt Publishing

Lauer, F., & Bloch, G. (2008). Incorporating prior knowledge in support vector machines for classification: A review. *Neurocomputing, 71*(7), 1578-1594. doi:10.1016/j.neucom.2007.04.010

Leading Regional Jet Operators. (2005). *Market Share Reporter*. Ed. R. Lazich and V. Burton. Detroit, MI: Gale. Retrieved from https://bi-gale-com.ezproxy.libproxy.db.erau.edu/essentials/article/GALE%7CI2502015786?u=embry&sid=summon

Lee, S., Park, W., & Jung, S. (2014). Fault detection of aircraft system with random forest algorithm and similarity measure. *The Scientific World Journal, 727359*-7. doi:10.1155/2014/727359

Lee, H., & Park, J. (2016). Comparative study on hazardous attitudes and safe operational behavior in airline pilots. *Journal of Air Transport Management, 54*, 70-79. doi:10.1016/j.jairtraman.2016.03.024

Li, L., Das, S., Hansman, R. J., Palacios, R., & Srivastava, A. N. (2015). Analysis of flight data using clustering techniques for detecting abnormal operations. *Journal of Aerospace Information Systems, 12*(9), 587-598. doi:10.2514/1.I010329

Li, L., Hansman, R.J., Palacios, R., & Welsh, R. (2016). Anomaly detection via a Gaussian mixture model for flight operation and safety monitoring. *Transportation Research Part C,* 45-57. doi.10.1016/j.trc.2016.01.007

Lv, H., Yu, J., & Zhu, T. (2018). A novel method of overrun risk measurement and assessment using large scale QAR data. *2018 IEEE Fourth International Conference on Big Data Computing Service and Applications* (pp. 213-220). doi:10.1109/BigDataService.2018.00039

Martinussen, D., & Hunter, D. (2010). *Aviation psychology and human factors*. Boca Raton, FL: CRC Press.

Matthews, B., Das, S., Bhaduri, K., Das, K., Martin, R., & Oza, N. (2013). Discovering anomalous aviation safety events using scalable data mining algorithms. *Journal of Aerospace Information Systems, 10*(10), 467-475. doi:10.2514/1.I010080

Maxson, R. W. (2018). *Prediction of airport arrival rates using data mining methods* (Doctoral Dissertation). Retrieved from https://commons.erau.edu/edt/419/

Mehta, D. P., & Sahni, S. (2018; 2017;). *Handbook of data structures and applications* (2nd ed.). Portland: Chapman and Hall/CRC. doi:10.1201/9781315119335

Mendes, H. (2012). *Study of mathematical algorithms to identify abnormal patterns in aircraft flight data* (Doctoral Dissertation). Institute of Superior Technology, University of Lisbon, Portugal. Retrieved from https://fenix.tecnico.ulisboa.pt/downloadFile/395144228216/TeseHM12Jun2012.pdf

Moriarty, D., & Jarvis, S. (2014). A systems perspective on the unstable approach in commercial aviation. *Reliability Engineering and System Safety, 131,* 197-202. doi:10.1016/j.ress.2014.06.019

Mozdzanowska, A., & Hansman, J. (2005). Growth and operating patterns of regional jets in the United States. *Journal of Aircraft, 42*(4), 858-864. doi:10.2514/1.11748

Mugtussidis, I. (2000). *Flight data processing techniques to identify unusual events* (Doctoral Dissertation). Retrieved from https://vtechworks.lib.vt.edu/bitstream/handle/10919/28095/phd.pdf?sequence=1&isAllowed=y

Moretti, L., Di Mascio, P., Nichele, S., & Cokorilo, O. (2018). Runway veer-off accidents: Quantitative risk assessment and risk reduction measures. *Safety Science, 104,* 157-163.doi:10.1016/j.ssci.2018.01.010

National Aeronautics and Space Administration [NASA]. (2012). *Sample flight data for 35 aircraft.* Retrieved from the NASA DASHlink website at https://c3.nasa.gov/DASHlink/projects/85/resources/?type=ds

National Transportation Safety Board [NTSB]. (2000). *Crash during landing, Federal Express Flight 14, McDonnell Douglas MD-11, N611FE, Newark, New Jersey, July 31, 1997* (Aircraft Accident Report NTSB/AAR-00/02). Washington, DC: Author. Retrieved from https://www.ntsb.gov/investigations/AccidentReports/Reports/AAR0002.pdf

National Transportation Safety Board [NTSB]. (2001). *Runway overrun during landing, American Airlines Flight 1420, McDonnell Douglas MD-82, N215AA, Little Rock, Arkansas, June 1, 1999* (Aircraft Accident Report NTSB/AAR-01/02). Washington, DC: Author. Retrieved from https://www.ntsb.gov/investigations/AccidentReports/Reports/AAR0102.pdf

National Transportation Safety Board [NTSB]. (2008). *Runway overrun during landing, Delta Connection Flight 6448, Embraer ERJ-170, N862RW, Cleveland, Ohio, February 18, 2007* (Aircraft Accident Report AAR-08/01). Washington, DC: Author. Retrieved from http://www.ntsb.gov/investigations/accidentreports/pages/aar0801.aspx

National Transportation Safety Board [NTSB]. (2014a). *Crash during a nighttime nonprecision instrument approach to landing, UPS Flight 1354, Airbus A300-600, N155UP, Birmingham, Alabama, August 14, 2013* (Aircraft Accident Report NTSB/AAR-14/02). Washington, DC: Author. Retrieved from https://www.ntsb.gov/investigations/AccidentReports/Reports/AAR1402.pdf

National Transportation Safety Board [NTSB]. (2014b). *Descent below visual glide-path and impact with seawall, Asiana Airlines Flight 214, Boeing 777-200ER, HL7742, San Francisco, California, July 6, 2013* (Aircraft Accident Report NTSB/AAR-14/01). Washington, DC: Author. Retrieved from https://www.ntsb.gov/investigations/AccidentReports/Reports/AAR1401.pdf

National Transportation Safety Board [NTSB]. (2016). *Runway overrun due to unstable approach, General Aviation, Embraer S A EMB-505, N32FL, Eden Prairie, Minnesota, August 5, 2013* (Aircraft Accident Report CEN13LA462). Washington, DC: Author. Retrieved from https://reports.aviation-safety.net/2013/20130805-1_E55P_N327FL.pdf

National Transportation Safety Board [NTSB]. (2019a). *Safety advocacy group: most wanted list of safety recommendations.* Washington, DC: Author. Retrieved from https://www.ntsb.gov/safety/mwl/Pages/mwl-4.aspx

National Transportation Safety Board [NTSB]. (2019b). *Stable approaches lead to safe landings.* (NTSTB Safety Alert 077, March 2019). Retrieved from https://www.ntsb.gov/safety/safety-alerts/Documents/SA-077.pdf

Nanduri, A. & Sherry, L. (2016). Anomaly detection in aircraft data using recurrent neural networks (RNN). *2016 Integrated Communications Navigation and Surveillance Conference* (pp.1-8). doi:10.1109/ICNSURV.2016.7486356

Oehling, J. & Barry, D. J. (2019). Using machine learning methods in airline flight data monitoring to generate new operational safety knowledge from existing data. *Safety Science, 114,* 89-104. doi:10.1016/j.ssci.2018.12.018

O'Hare, D. (1990). Pilots' perception of risks and hazards in general aviation. *Aviation, Space, and Environmental Medicine, 61*(7), 599.

Orasanu, J., Davison, J., Ciavarelli, A., Cohen, M., Fischer, U., & Slovic, P. (2001). The many faces of risk in aviation decision making. *Human Factors and Ergonomics Society Annual Meeting Proceedings, 45*(4), 307-310. doi:10.1177/154193120104500409

Patel, T., & Thompson, W. (2013). *Data mining from A to Z: Better insights, new opportunities* (White Paper). Retrieved from SAS® website at http://www.datascienceassn.org/sites/default/files/Data%20Mining%20from%20A%20to%20Z.pdf

Paul, J., & Dupont, P. (2015). Inferring statistically significant features from random forests. *Neurocomputing, 150,* 471-480. doi:10.1016/j.neucom.2014.07.067

Puranik, T. G., & Mavris, D. N. (2018). Anomaly detection in general-aviation operations using energy metrics and flight-data records. *Journal of Aerospace Information Systems, 15*(1), 22-35. doi:10.2514/1.I010582

Ravindran, A., & Meht, D. (2018). Data structures for big data stores. In D. Mehta & S Sahni (Eds.), *Handbook of data structures and applications (2nd ed.), (pp. 983-995).* Portland: CRC Press.

Rogerson, E. C., & Lambert, J. H. (2012). Prioritizing risks via several expert perspectives with application to runway safety. *Reliability Engineering and System Safety, 103,* 22-34. doi:10.1016/j.ress.2012.03.001

Sarma, K. S. (2013). *Predictive modeling with SAS enterprise miner: Practical solutions for business applications* (2nd ed.). Cary, NC: SAS Institute.

Sherry, L., Wang, Z., Kourdali, H. K., & Shortle, J. (2013). *Big data analysis of irregular operations: Aborted approaches and their underlying factors. 2013*

Integrated Communications, Navigation and Surveillance Conference (pp. 1-10). doi:10.1109/ICNSurv.2013.6548548

Shi, D., Guan, J., Zurada, J., & Manikas, A. (2017). A data-mining approach to identification of risk factors in safety management systems. *Journal of Management Information Systems, 34*(4), 1054-1081. doi:10.1080/07421 222.2017.1394056

Shish, K., Kaneshige, J., Acosta, D., Schuet, S., Lombaerts, T., Martin, L., & Madavan, A. N. (2017). Aircraft mode and energy-state prediction, assessment, and alerting. *Journal of Guidance, Control, and Dynamics, 40*(4), 804-816. doi:10.2514/1.G001765

Singh, V., Gupta, R. K., Sevakula, R. K., & Verma, N. K. (2016). Comparative analysis of Gaussian mixture model, logistic regression and random forest for big data classification using map reduce. *11th International Conference on Industrial and Information Systems* (pp. 333-338). doi:10.1109/ICIINFS.2016.8262961

Smart, E. (2011). *Detecting abnormalities in aircraft flight data and ranking their impact on the flight.* (Doctoral Dissertation). University of Portsmouth, United Kingdom). Retrieved from https://researchportal.port.ac.uk/portal/en/theses/detecting-abnormalities-in-aircraft-flight-data-and-ranking-their-impact-on-the-flight(d9678b70-41e6-459a-82fb-ba2d12a0f971).html

Takahashi, T. T., & Delisle, M. (2018). (Un) stabilized approach-an introduction to dynamic flight conditions during takeoff and landing climb. In *2018 Aviation Technology, Integration, and Operations Conference* (p. 3500). doi:10.2514/6.2018-35

Thompson, M. (2017). Using ADS-B big data analysis to create stable approach models. *Journal of Air Traffic Control.* Retrieved from: https://trid.trb.org/view/1473370

Tong, C., Yin, X., Wang, S., & Zheng, Z. (2018). A novel deep learning method for aircraft landing speed prediction based on cloud-based sensor data. *Future Generation Computer Systems, 88*, 552-558. doi:10.1016/j.future.2018.06.023

Treder, B., & Crane, B. (2004). *Application of insightful corporation data mining algorithms to FOQA data at JetBlue airways.* Flight Safety Foundation Report. Retrieved from https://flightsafety.org/files/FOQA_data_mining_report.pdf.

Truong, D., Friend, M. A., & Chen, H. (2018). Applications of business analytics in predicting flight on-time performance in a complex and dynamic system. *Transportation Journal, 57*(1), 24-52. doi:10.5325/transportationj.57.1.0024

Tufféry, S. (2011). *Data mining and statistics for decision making.* West Sussex, United Kingdom: John Wiley & Sons.

Vértesy, D. (2017). Preconditions, windows of opportunity and innovation strategies: Successive leadership changes in the regional jet industry. *Research Policy, 46*(2), 388-403. doi:10.1016/j.respol.2016.09.011

Vogt, W. P., Gardner, D. C., Haeffele, L. M., & Vogt, E. R. (2014). *Selecting the right analyses for your data: Quantitative, qualitative, and mixed methods*. Guilford Publications.

Walker, G. (2017). Redefining the incidents to learn from: Safety science insights acquired on the journey from black boxes to flight data monitoring. *Safety Science, 99*, 14-22. doi:10.1016/j.ssci.2017.05.010

Wang, Z. (2016). *A methodology for nowcasting unstable approaches* (Doctoral dissertation). Retrieved from ProQuest Dissertations Publishing. (10135073)

Wang, L., Ren, Y., & Wu, C. (2018). Effects of flare operation on landing safety: A study based on ANOVA of real flight data. *Safety Science, 102*, 14-25. doi:10.1016/j.ssci.2017.09.027

Wang, L., Wu, C., & Sun, R. (2014). An analysis of flight quick access recorder (QAR) data and its applications in preventing landing incidents. *Reliability Engineering and System Safety, 127*, 86-96. doi:10.1016/j.ress.2014.03.013

Wong, D. K. Y., Pitfield, D. E., & Humphreys, I. M. (2005). The impact of regional jets on air service at selected US airports and markets. *Journal of Transport Geography, 13*(2), 151-163. doi:10.1016/j.jtrangeo.2004.04.012

You, X., Ji, M., & Han, H. (2013). The effects of risk perception and flight experience on airline pilots' locus of control with regard to safety operation behaviors. *Accident Analysis and Prevention, 57*, 131-139. doi:10.1016/j.aap.2013.03.036

Zhao, X. B., Bin, L. I., & Wang, C. G. (2017). There is a gold mine in flight data: A framework of data Mining in Civil Aviation. *DEStech Transactions on Social Science, Education and Human Science*. Retrieved from http://www.dpi-proceedings.com/index.php/dtssehs/article/view/12896/12429

ACKNOWLEDGEMENTS

I must first acknowledge my parents, Edwin and DeAnn Odisho, for instilling upon me the values of education and hard work, and for providing me with the opportunity to achieve and succeed. Without the love and support of my wife, Bettina, my ability to multitask between spending time with my family, flying full time, and conducting aviation research would not be possible. USAF test pilot school colleague and NASA astronaut COL G. Zamka, USMC provided a great example of hard work, determination and self-discipline. Finally, from my academic mentor, Dr. Dothang Truong, I learned how to combine my passion for aviation safety with academic rigor, research, and scholarship.

This project would not have never departed the gate without the expertise, guidance and advice of several literary experts. I want to express my sincere gratitude to Dr. Karlene Pettit for her assisting me in getting my book project to the active runway as well as introducing me to the absolutely superb editor and literary expert Mr. Nathan Everett of Elder Road Books. I also want to thank retired airline captain and founder of Eyewitness Animations, Captain Jack Suchocki and team of designers, led by Mr. Martin Merryman, for their generosity in the use of the Asiana 214 re-creation that is depicted on the cover. Thank you one and all. Semper Fidelis!

ABOUT THE AUTHOR

Edwin (Ed) Odisho is a captain for a major US airline. Prior to his commercial airline career, he was a United States Marine Corps aviator for over 11 years and graduated from the United States Air Force Test Pilot School at Edwards AFB, CA. He has flown more than 40 aircraft types to include fighters, transports, helicopters, and gliders. Ed is also type rated on the Boeing 707, 727, 757, 767, 777, Lockheed L382, and Airbus 320 aircraft. Ed has completed Bachelor and Master degrees in Aerospace Engineering and Aviation Systems respectively, and has earned a Ph.D. in Aviation, with subspecialties in Aviation Safety and Human Factors. Ed is also husband to Bettina and father to two daughters. He enjoys running, reading, photography, and cycling.

www.ingramcontent.com/pod-product-compliance
Lightning Source LLC
Chambersburg PA
CBHW050323120526
44592CB00014B/2033